AMERICAN HISTORY

VOLUME VII: WAR OF THE REVOLUTION

JACOB ABBOTT

SANDYCROFT PUBLISHING

PREFACE

It is the design of this work to narrate, in a clear, simple, and intelligible manner, the leading events connected with the history of our country, from the earliest periods, down, as nearly as practicable, to the present time. The several volumes will be illustrated with all necessary maps and with numerous engravings, and the work is intended to comprise, in a distinct and connected narrative, all that it is essential for the general reader to understand in respect to the subject of it, while for those who have time for more extended studies, it may serve as an introduction to other and more copious sources of information.

The author hopes also that the work may be found useful to the young, in awakening in their minds an interest in the history of their country, and a desire for further instruction in respect to it. While it is doubtless true that such a subject can be really grasped only by minds in some degree mature, still the author believes that many young persons, especially such as are intelligent and thoughtful in disposition and character, may derive both entertainment and instruction from a perusal of these pages.

Preparation for war.

WAR OF THE REVOLUTION

CHAPTER I
THE CONTINENTAL CONGRESS

VIRGINIA AND MASSACHUSETTS

The war of the American Revolution was conducted, on the part of the colonies, by a body of men formed of delegates from each of the different provinces, and called the Continental Congress.

The provinces of Virginia and Massachusetts took the lead in the formation of this congress, though they were not the first to propose it. It is said that the first public proposal that the colonies should form some union, so as to enable them to act together in the general contest with the mother country, was made about the middle of May, 1774, at a town meeting in Rhode Island. Four days afterward a committee of a town meeting in Philadelphia made the same recommendation, and similar action was taken, in May and June, by various towns in nearly all the other provinces.

Thus the general government of the United States, which has since risen to so high a position of greatness and power, had its origin in town meetings. It was from these little rootlets that the mighty tree originally sprung, as it is by them, or by the democratic principles of self-government and equal rights which grow and thrive in these small and scattered organizations, that it is still nourished and sustained.

It was, however, by the legislatures of Massachusetts and Virginia that the first steps were taken toward carrying the proposal into effect, though the legislatures of all the other colonies very readily concurred in the measure. The place in which the meetings were held was Philadelphia; and the first meeting took place September 5th, 1774, some months before the actual commencement of the war.

DIFFICULTIES IN THE WAY OF FORMING ANY UNION OF THE COLONIES

Previous to about the year 1773, the several colonies were entirely separate and distinct, it being the evident policy of the government to bind them individually as closely as possible to the mother country, and to keep them, at the same time, entirely disconnected from one another, so as to prevent anything like concert of action among them in case of any disagreement or difficulty between them and the government at home.

The colonies submitted without objection to this policy so long as no difficulty occurred, but when the question of the taxation of the American people through the action of Parliament, which was composed wholly of representatives of the English people at home, instead of through that of the colonial legislatures, which were composed of their own representatives, began to come under discussion, it was found that all the colonies had a common cause against the mother country, and a disposition to form some sort of union which would enable them to act in concert began at once to appear.

It was very difficult, however, to carry any plan of union into effect, for the governors of the colonies were appointed by the ministry, and according to the charters or other fundamental laws of the several provinces, the governor, though he could not take any part, directly, in the proceedings of the assemblies, could nevertheless so far control the times and places of their meetings, that it was almost impossible for them to transact any business in them which he disapproved.

If they brought forward and began to discuss any subject or plan which he objected to, he had only to send in immediately a special messenger and dissolve the assembly—when all their power to act legally, as a legislative body, was at an end.

LIABILITY TO A CHARGE OF TREASON

Besides these difficulties in the way of effecting any regular and legal action by the constituted authorities of any colony for forming a combination with the others, the people knew that the persons who should attempt any action of this kind might subject themselves to a charge of conspiracy or treason—on the ground that they were attempting to organize a lawless confederation, for the purpose of resisting the government. A few years, or rather a few months, after this time, when the war was on the eve of breaking out, the leaders of the resistance paid very little regard to any considerations of this kind. They had by that time gone so far that they considered it of little moment whether the government should charge them with treason or not. But at the commencement of the troubles they were more cautious, as it was very proper that they should be. They hoped to induce the mother country to abandon its claim to tax them by votes of Parliament, without an open rupture, and they were accordingly very desirous to confine their resistance and opposition, for a time at least, to such measures as should be strictly and indisputably legal.

APPOINTMENT OF COMMITTEES OF CORRESPONDENCE

In accordance with this view, the plan which they first adopted was the appointment of what were called Committees of Correspondence. However illegal it might be to attempt to institute any combined action among the colonies, there certainly could not be anything treasonable, they reasoned, in writing letters for the purpose of communicating or gaining information, or in appointing committees to write them. Virginia took the lead in this measure, and the other colonies immediately followed. The governors did all they could to prevent even this action, and in some cases dissolved the assemblies in time to prevent the proposed committees from being chosen by them. But in such cases the people themselves held meetings and appointed the committees, and in this manner in the course of a few months there was a regular and semi-official channel of intercommunication among all the colonies, through which the state of public sentiment and the progress of events in each was made known promptly and fully to all the rest. This system, while it continued, had a very powerful influence in promoting a common understanding among all the colonies, and in preparing the way for the more intimate union which followed.

ORGANIZATION OF THE CONTINENTAL CONGRESS

At length, when, in consequence of the destruction of the tea in Boston Harbor, the British government, in order to punish the people for the insubordinate spirit which they had manifested by that act, closed the port, thus destroying the business of the town, and reducing the great mass of the people to poverty and distress at a blow, the indignation of the people in all the provinces was so aroused, that they everywhere began to be prepared to adopt bolder measures. The legislature of Virginia passed resolutions declaring that the cause of Massachusetts was the cause of all the colonies, and that in order to enable them to maintain their cause in a decisive manner, some more effectual plan for uniting their councils than had yet been adopted, was required.

Encouraged by this open stand taken by Virginia, and also by the manifestations of public sentiment in nearly all the other provinces, given by the action of the various town meetings already referred to, the Massachusetts assembly at once voted to recommend to all the provinces to appoint delegates to a Continental Congress, to he convened at Philadelphia, the most central point. This was on the 5th of June, 1774, and in order to allow time for the full consideration of this proposal, for the appointment of delegates by all the colonies, they proposed that the time for the meeting of the congress should be in three months from that date, namely, the 5th of September.

The governors both of Virginia and of Massachusetts were very earnest in their efforts to prevent this action, and did their utmost to arrest it, but they did not succeed. The legislatures, partly by rapid action, and partly by a little artifice, contrived to defeat their efforts, and to accomplish the work.

PROFESSED OBJECT OF THE PROPOSED CONGRESS

In the resolution passed by Massachusetts recommending the congress—the purpose of convening such an assembly was stated to be "For concerting proper measures for the recovery and establishment of the just rights and liberties of the Americans, and for the restoration of that union and harmony between Great Britain and America, most ardently desired by all good men."

This language was used in part, no doubt, to defend the formation of the proposed congress from the charge of being a treasonable measure. There certainly could be nothing treasonable, it would seem, in a meeting of gentlemen from different provinces, for the purpose of consulting on the best means of restoring union and harmony between the provinces and the mother country.

There is no doubt, too, that this language, in respect to a large portion of those who adopted it, was sincere. The plan of separating altogether from the mother country, and establishing a distinct and separate commonwealth in America, was yet entertained by comparatively few.

APPOINTMENT OF DELEGATES TO THE CONGRESS BY THE OTHER PROVINCES

Nearly all the provinces fell in at once with the Massachusetts plan of appointing delegates. The governors everywhere did their utmost to prevent this, but they were unable to succeed. In some cases they prevented the legislatures from acting, but then the people themselves, in a more informal manner, made the appointments, and in due time the assembly was convened.

PLACE OF MEETING OF THE FIRST CONGRESS

The place decided upon for the first meeting of the congress, was a hall in Philadelphia, known as Carpenter's Hall. It was a plain building, with one large room below, and several smaller ones in the story above. These last were used by the congress for committee rooms and for other similar purposes.

FIRST MEETING OF THE MEMBERS

The number of members that had been appointed by the different provinces was fifty-four. They were all men of great prominence and note in their several provinces, and well known to each other by name and reputation; and many of them had been in habits of correspondence with each other in respect to public affairs, having

PATRICK HENRY

The person that rose at last to address the assembly was Patrick Henry.

Patrick Henry was a Virginian—a man of great eloquence, and renowned throughout the country for the very able and powerful speeches which he had made in the Virginia House of Burgesses, as the legislative assembly of that province was called. These speeches had been read all over the land, and the name of Patrick Henry was everywhere known. But still, among the members of the congress, scarcely anyone personally knew the man.

He was a very grave-looking personage, and his countenance wore an earnest and thoughtful expression; but his appearance was plain and unpretending, and he was without any of those indications of dress in the way of colored cloths, ruffles, and powdered wigs, with which men of wealth or of high position were accustomed to adorn themselves in those days. Indeed, some of the delegates expressed a feeling of mortification that so insignificant a man should be the first to address so august an assembly on such an occasion.

The moment that he began to speak, however, opinions were suddenly changed. There was a charm in the tones of his voice, and an impressive eloquence in his modes of expression, that at once aroused universal attention.

"Who is it?" "Who is it?" asked the members of each other, in whispers—inquiring in vain on each side of them, and before and behind.

At length, however, the response "Patrick Henry!" "Patrick Henry!" began to circulate along the seats; and then very soon every member assumed an attitude of profound attention.

The speech was a very able and earnest vindication of the indefeasible right of the people of the colonies to the control which they claimed over their own internal policy, and an urgent call upon Congress to organize a firm, united, and vigorous resistance to the encroachments of the British crown. It produced a very profound sensation.

Principle of Representation Adopted

The actual business of the congress was not fully entered upon until the third day. The first day was occupied in the preliminary proceedings above referred to, and the second was devoted to drawing up and adopting rules for regulating the proceedings. The most important of these rules was the one determining the manner in which the voting power should be apportioned among the members. The different provinces varied very much in wealth and population, and the number of delegates, too, which had been sent, differed greatly, while these two variations did not correspond at all with each other. If the comparative population of the several provinces could have been ascertained, it would seem to have been just to allow each one a number of votes proportioned to the number of the people. But there were no means of determining this question, and so it was finally decided to allow to each province one vote on all questions to be passed upon. What this vote should be in each delegation was of course determined by the majority of the delegation itself at a preliminary balloting among themselves.

Question of Opening the Session with Prayer

The congress became finally ready to proceed to the transaction of business on the third day; and it had been proposed on the preceding evening, that before actually commencing the momentous work before them, they should unitedly and publicly implore the blessing of God upon their counsels; and that, accordingly, some clergyman should be invited to open the session with prayer. This proposal was objected to by some of the members, on the ground that there was so great a diversity of religious sentiment in the congress, and so many religious persuasions represented among the members—Episcopalians, Quakers, Baptists, Congregationalists, and Presbyterians—that they could not all join in an act of worship in any one form.

To this the venerable Samuel Adams from Boston replied, that he for one could join in a prayer from any clergyman of piety and virtue, who was a friend of his country, whatever his religious persuasion might be. And he immediately made a motion, that Mr. Duché,[1] who was a prominent Episcopal minister of Philadelphia, might be desired to read prayers before Congress on the following morning.

When the members thus heard a venerable delegate from Massachusetts—representing a people whose ancestors, as they believed, had been driven from England by the intolerance of the Episcopal Church, and who still felt a special repugnance against everything like prelacy in church government, and to all written forms in religious worship—propose an Episcopal minister for this duty, no one seemed disposed to make any further objection, and the motion was carried. The president, Mr. Randolph, waited upon Mr. Duché, and the arrangement was made.

The First Prayer in Congress

The next morning Mr. Duché appeared at the appointed time, dressed in his canonicals, and accompanied by his clerk, according to the usages of his church, as it was very proper that he should be. He would not do the members the injustice to suppose, that in inviting him—an Episcopal minister—to conduct their devotions, they expected him to leave his clerical office, or anything essentially pertaining to it, according to the rules and usages of his communion, behind him.

Mr. Duché read the prayers proper to the occasion, and the portion of the Psalter pertaining to the day, which was the 7th of September. The portion read was the thirty-fifth Psalm.

After having done this, the minister, unexpectedly to everyone, commenced an extemporaneous prayer, adapted more closely to the circumstances of the occasion. He prayed for Congress, for the province of Massachusetts Bay, and especially for the town of Boston, with such fervor and pathos, and in language so elegant and sublime, that it deeply impressed everyone present, and produced a very profound sensation.

The solemn excitement which was occasioned by this prayer, especially the portion which related to Boston, was greatly increased by certain intelligence relating to the progress of events in that town,

---

[1]Pronounced Dushay.

which had arrived the day before, and had renewed afresh the deep interest which was everywhere felt in what was there transpiring.

During the prayer it was observed that one only of the members kneeled. That one was George Washington. He was one of the members from Virginia.

DIFFERENCE OF OPINION AMONG THE MEMBERS IN RESPECT TO THE COURSE TO BE PURSUED

Although no regular account of the discussions and debates which took place in this first congress has been preserved, it is well known that there was great difference of opinion among the members in respect to the course which it was best that the country should pursue.

The younger and more ardent men were in favor of very decisive action. They wished to bid open defiance at once to the power of Great Britain, to declare the provinces separated finally and forever from the mother country, and to establish an independent government. This would, of course, lead to a terrible and probably long-protracted war with the most formidable military and naval power on earth— but they were ready for such a war.

The older and more prudent men were not prepared to take this step. Some of them thought that separation must be in the end the result of the quarrel, and they ardently wished that it might be so—but they did not think that the time had yet come for them to proclaim it. They did not know whether the country was prepared for such a step; and then, moreover, they thought that by making one more last effort to induce the British government to relinquish their claims to absolute domination in America, they should place themselves and the justice of their cause in a better position before the world, and make their final success more sure.

Others, it seems, were opposed to any policy whatever that looked toward a separation from Britain, or even to doing anything which should tend to bring on war. One of the speakers who entertained these views, undertook to show how entirely exposed the country was to the overwhelming power of England.

"All our largest and most important towns," said he, "are situated along the Atlantic seaboard, on rivers or harbors entirely open to

English ships of war, by which they can all be easily and totally destroyed."

To which another speaker replied that those towns were all built of wood, of bricks, and of other more or less perishable materials, which, when once destroyed, could be easily replaced by an industrious and energetic people. The country, he said, was full of beds of clay and of growing timber, from which new cities could easily be built. But, if their rights and liberties, he added, were once surrendered to foreign control, and the people reduced into subjection to a foreign power, the loss and injury could never be repaired.

FINAL DECISION OF THE CONGRESS

The result of the deliberations of the congress was in favor, for the time being, of very moderate measures. Their action was confined, almost exclusively, to the issuing of a number of addresses to various classes of persons and public bodies, the main object of which was to lay the case of the American people fully and fairly before the world, in its true and proper light. The principal of these communications were the following:

1. A general declaration of rights in behalf of the American people, specifying precisely what they claimed as the inherent and indefeasible rights of all subjects of the British Empire.

2. A memorial to the king of England, setting forth the grounds of complaint which the people of his colonies in America had against his majesty's government, and asking for redress.

3. An appeal to the Parliament and to the people of England, calling upon them to sympathize and take part with their fellow subjects in America, in withstanding the encroachments of power and maintaining unimpaired the liberties, rights, and privileges secured by the ancient laws and usages of the realm to every British subject, and which all had a joint and common interest in defending.

4. An address to the people of America, calling upon them to be united and firm in defense of their rights; and, while avoiding all rash, or hasty, or intemperate measures, to be firm and immovable in their determination never to yield to any attempt to deprive them of the political rights and privileges which they and their forefathers

had always enjoyed, and which were secured not only by the British constitution to all the subjects of the British empire, but by the laws of God and of nature, to every human being.

5. And finally a series of addresses to the people of the provinces of Canada, New Brunswick, and Nova Scotia, that were settled, in a great measure, by the French, urging them to join the English colonies in their efforts to secure rights common to all. These last addresses failed to produce any decisive effect. The native populations of those provinces were French by nationality and Catholic in faith; and they had little fellow-feeling with the spirit of liberty and independence which prevailed in the colonies of English origin. The small proportion of English people that these northern colonies contained, consisted to a great extent of men in office, and of persons more or less connected with and dependent upon them, and they were very naturally inclined to take sides with the government in the contest that was arising.

AN APPEAL TO ARMS CONDITIONALLY RECOMMENDED

During the time that Congress had been in session, things had been drawing rapidly toward a crisis in Massachusetts. General Gage, the commander of the British military forces in America, had been appointed governor of the province. He had assembled a considerable number of troops in Boston, had thrown up intrenchments across the neck which connected the peninsula with the mainland, and which afforded the only mode of access to the town in those days, as there were then no bridges.

He had begun also to take measures for seizing and securing such depots of arms and munitions of war as the colony possessed. The whole country was looking with great interest to the course which events were taking in Boston; and a regular express was established between Boston and Philadelphia during the session of Congress, to carry the intelligence of what transpired as regularly and as rapidly as possible to and fro.

The immediate cause of all this special excitement in Boston was that that town, and the whole province, in fact, had given great offense to Parliament and to the English government, by destroying the tea of the East India Company in Boston Harbor, rather than pay any taxes upon it not assessed by their own legislature, and by other similar acts of insubordination; and Parliament had accordingly passed acts for shutting up the port of Boston entirely, so as to destroy the business of the town, and also for entirely remodeling the government of the province, so as to deprive the people of a large part of the limited share in the government which they had previously enjoyed.

Under this state of things, Congress, toward the close of the session, passed a resolution, approving of the resistance made by the people of Massachusetts to the late acts of Parliament, and declaring that if General Gage should attempt to carry those acts into effect by force, all America ought to unite in supporting Massachusetts in her opposition.

DISSOLUTION OF CONGRESS

Having adopted these several measures, and some others which it is not necessary to particularize here, Congress prepared to bring the session to a close. Before doing so, however, a vote was passed recommending to the several provinces to make arrangements for a new congress, and naming the 10th of May, of the ensuing year, as the proper time for it to be convened, unless the grievances of the American people should before that time be redressed, in which case it might not be necessary that it should be convened at all.

And inasmuch as circumstances might occur making it desirable that a new congress should be assembled before that time, they recommended that the several provinces should proceed to elect the new members without delay, so that the assembly might be convened at any time when the emergency should occur requiring it.

The first congress having thus prepared the way for the calling, in due time, of a second, voted its own dissolution; and the members, bidding each other farewell, with many mingled hopes and forebodings, proceeded to their several homes.

IMMEDIATE RESULTS OF THE ACTION OF THE FIRST CONGRESS

The measures adopted by the first congress, so far as they aimed at a peaceable arrangement of the difficulties between the colonies and the mother country failed of success. Indeed the only effect of them was to hasten the preparations on both sides for a vigorous prosecution of hostilities. The address sent to the people of America exerted a powerful influence in uniting them together, and greatly strengthened their determination to resist the encroachments of the British government to the last extremity.

THE CONTINENTAL CONGRESS

On the other hand the remonstrances and appeals addressed to the British government and people, failed altogether in inducing the ministry to alter their course, while still they awakened the sympathy and excited the admiration of many men in England of the highest rank and influence.

PARLIAMENT REFUSES TO RECEIVE THE MEMORIAL ADDRESSED TO IT BY CONGRESS

When the memorials addressed by the congress to the government and the people of England arrived in that country, a committee which had been appointed by Congress for that purpose made application to Parliament for a hearing. The celebrated Benjamin Franklin was the most prominent person on this committee. He and his colleagues tendered a petition to the house, stating that they were directed by the American Continental Congress to present a memorial from it, the contents of which it was in their power to illustrate by much important information, and asking to be heard at the bar of the house according to the established custom in Parliament in cases where a person not a member desires to address the house on any subject, and the house accords him permission to do so.

The house in this case refused to grant the petition to be heard, or to receive the memorial. The excuse for the refusal was, that the complaints of the Americans were only fancied or pretended grievances, that they had no just ground of remonstrance whatever, and that the Continental Congress from which the memorial emanated was an entirely illegal, if not treasonable, assembly.

Thus the only immediate result produced by the deliberations and actions of the first American congress was to excite still higher the imperious resentment of the British government against the refractory colonists, and also to hasten the union and organization of the colonists themselves, for the purpose of resistance, and to fix and strengthen their determination to resist, at all hazards, and to the last extremity.

CHAPTER II
EXPULSION OF THE BRITISH FROM BOSTON

The Fall and Winter of 1775

The Continental Congress closed its session about the end of October, and the autumn and winter passed away without any open collision, though the excitement throughout the country was very great, and was constantly increasing. The party disposed to take sides with the British government was strong enough in some of the provinces to embarrass the action of the people for a time, but as the government went on adopting more and more stringent measures against the colonies, which had the effect only to arouse the resentment of the Americans to a higher and higher pitch, and to unite them more and more closely in a determination to resist, it gradually became evident to all that the contest would soon result in open war.

The Battle of Lexington

As related in the preceding volume of this series, the first actual conflict took place at Lexington, in Massachusetts, in consequence of a detachment of troops having been sent out to Concord, a town a little way beyond Lexington, where the government of Massachusetts had commenced making a collection of military stores in anticipation of the war.[1]

The object of the expedition was only very partially successful, as but a portion of the stores were destroyed—the rest having been hastily carried away and concealed by the people—and the troops sent out were followed and harassed incessantly on their return to Boston, so that they lost in killed, wounded, and prisoners, nearly

---

[1]See map on following page.

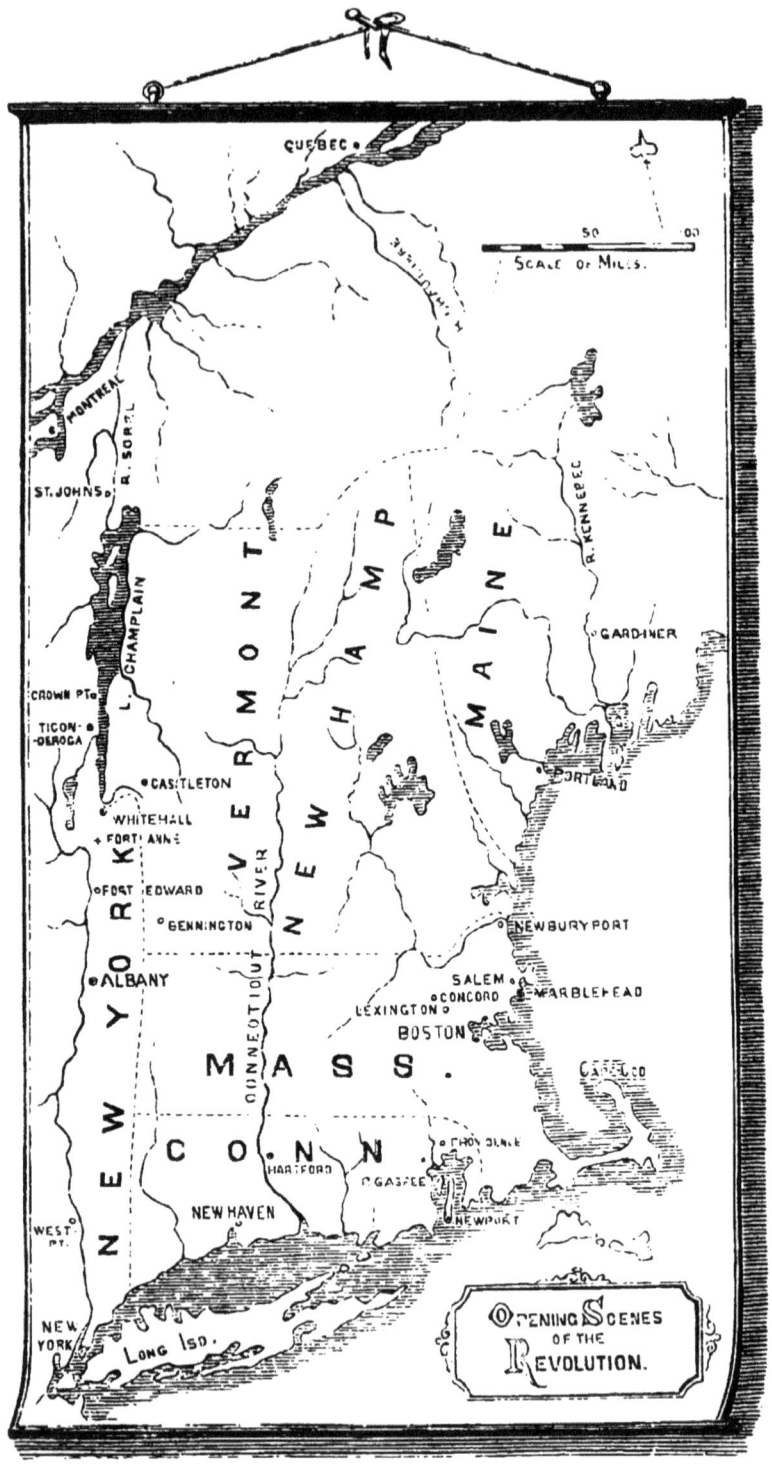

three hundred men. The whole country was, moreover, aroused by the tidings of the conflict, and the most vigorous preparations were made everywhere for immediate war. In Connecticut, in New Hampshire, and in other neighboring provinces, bodies of men were armed and organized, and led at once toward Boston. The country people seized and put in order such arms as they could find, and those that were too old or too young to march to the scene of the conflict, aided in equipping and in fitting out the sons and the brothers who were to go. Many a farmer's fireside was transformed into an arsenal for the assembling and making ready of arms and munitions of war. All were engaged at once in warlike preparations: rolling bandages, repairing clothes and accoutrements and casting bullets for the guns.[1]

Boston Besieged

The young and middle-aged men enrolled themselves rapidly as volunteers, under officers who were chosen by the men themselves, or who had previously been appointed by the provincial assemblies, and as fast as they were organized they set off in detachments for the environs of Boston.

In Connecticut, General Putnam, a man who had acquired great distinction by his indomitable bravery in former wars, but was now living quietly on his farm, heard the news while ploughing in his field. It is said he left his plough in the furrow, mounted one of the horses of his team in his working dress, took his sword at the door of his house, and placing himself at the head of a body of volunteers raised in his neighborhood, set off at once for the scene of action.

This spirit prevailed to such an extent that in three days the British troops, who had in the meantime shut themselves up in Boston, were hemmed in there by an army of twenty or thirty thousand men.

Gradual Organization of the American Army

This force could however scarcely yet be called an army, for it was formed of heterogeneous masses of men, suddenly assembled, very

---

[1]See p. ii.

imperfectly armed and equipped, not regularly officered, and totally without discipline. For some time all was confusion, and in a very few days, when it appeared that there was no immediate danger of a renewal of hostilities, great numbers left the field and went home again, some with, and some without, good reason.

During all this time there was great anxiety lest the troops in Boston should make a sortie and attack them. But they did not. The absent men soon returned, or others came to supply their places. Order was gradually produced out of the confusion. Officers were appointed, the regular routine of discipline was established, and before many days a line of cantonments was formed, extending in a semi-circle all around the town, on the land side, for a distance of twenty miles, from Charlestown, on the north, to Roxbury, on the south, and General Gage found himself closely shut up and besieged by so large a force as to make it hopeless for him to attempt to attack them.

STATE OF THINGS WITHIN THE TOWN

The people within the town were thrown by this condition of things into a state of great agitation and alarm. General Gage at once closed all the avenues of egress, and would not allow anyone to leave the place, nor would he permit the people to hold any communication with the neighboring towns, or to receive supplies of any kind. The whole population had been suddenly caught as in a trap, and unless there could be some way of obtaining speedy relief, hundreds of families saw imminently impending over them all the horrors of absolute want, if not of actual starvation.

General Gage himself was, moreover, somewhat alarmed at his own situation, being apprehensive that in case an attack should be made upon him by the army without, the people of the town might, in their desperation, rise upon the troops and massacre them. So he concluded soon to offer the townspeople a compromise.

THE COMPROMISE

The compromise which he offered was in this wise. He sought an interview with the selectmen, and informed them that he, on his part, would do no injury to the town, and no violence to any of the people, provided that the people themselves would behave peaceably; and that if the inhabitants generally would bring in all the arms and ammunition which they had in their possession—each parcel properly enveloped and marked with the owner's name—and deliver them to be stored in Faneuil Hall, they should remain there under the charge of the selectmen, and in due time should be returned to the owners; and that after the arms were so deposited any of the inhabitants who wished should be permitted to leave the town with their families and their effects.

General Gage's motive for making this proposal was of course to disarm the town of Boston and relieve himself of all fear of an uprising of the inhabitants within his lines, to cooperate with any attack which might be made from without. The people were extremely unwilling to yield to him this advantage, but they had no alternative except absolute starvation, and they voted, in town meeting, to accept the terms.

The arms were accordingly collected and deposited in Faneuil Hall, and then, for a time, passes were given to all who desired them. Great numbers of the inhabitants left the city, a large proportion of the refugees consisting of families in a state of extreme destitution and distress.

The people of the surrounding towns immediately made systematic arrangements for receiving and taking care of these fugitives. A certain number were allotted to each town, where they were provided with shelter and with the means of satisfying their most urgent wants. The number thus succored amounted to more than five thousand.

THE TORIES

The inhabitants of Boston were not by any means unanimous in their disposition to resist the mother country. A considerable number adhered to the government, and these, while the others were leaving the city, began to enroll themselves as soldiers in order to offer their services to General Gage. About two hundred, it is said, thus took up arms and joined themselves to the British forces. These men, it seems, as is usual in such cases, were more bitter and unsparing in their hostility to the insurgents than the British troops themselves, whom they volunteered to aid. They soon began to make objections to the policy of allowing so many of the inhabitants to leave the lines. They represented to General Gage that the besiegers, as soon as they found that all their friends had escaped from the town, would bombard and burn it; and that he ought to retain a sufficient number of them, especially of the women and children, to serve as hostages.

But General Gage had given his promise that if the people would deliver up their arms, he would allow them to depart in peace. This they had done, and how could he now violate his pledged word?

He was, however, convinced of the reality of the danger which the Tories pointed out to him, and finally concluded substantially to follow their advice. He would not positively refuse passes to men who applied for them, but he began to encumber the passes with various vexatious conditions and hindrances; and he made such arrangements that the different members of the same family were obliged to go at different times, and in different ways, so as to become separated from each other, and also to be separated from their household goods and other property; and these difficulties and embarrassments had the effect of preventing many families from going at all, while he could still claim that he had not violated his agreement, but only made such arrangements for carrying it into effect as military necessity required.

The Americans were, of course, greatly exasperated at these proceedings.

TICONDEROGA AND CROWN POINT

As the news of General Gage's attempt to seize the stores at Concord spread throughout the country, and after the first impulse which prompted the sending of all the men that could be raised to the vicinity of Boston had in some measure subsided, some thinking men began to consider whether it was not now the turn of the colonists to try the plan of the seizure of stores and munitions of war.

By looking at the map at the head of this chapter, the reader will observe that there is an almost continuous valley extending north from the seaboard at New York to the banks of the St. Lawrence, in Canada—as indicated by the course of the Hudson River—the line of the Lakes George and Champlain, and the river Sorel. This valley had been for many years the principal channel of communication between Canada and the colonies on the Atlantic coast, and had been the scene of many military operations in the wars which the English had waged with the Indians on the northern frontier, and with the French when the French were in possession of Canada.

During this time two strong fortresses had been constructed on the shores of the narrow part of Lake Champlain, to guard the pass. These fortresses were at Ticonderoga and Crown Point. They were garrisoned at this time by British troops, and a considerable quantity of military stores had been collected there.

The possession of these forts, involving, as it did, the possession of the pass which they commanded, enabled the British to cut off all communication between Canada and the other colonies, and thus to prevent the Canadians from joining them, if they had been disposed to do so, and also put it in the power of the British to bring an armed force down from Canada by that route, and thus attack the Atlantic colonies in the rear.

Secret Expeditions Fitted Out

The Americans understanding this state of things, saw very soon the desirableness of sending an expedition at once to seize these forts, before the British should have time to strengthen the garrisons.

No less than three several parties were formed for this purpose, in a great measure independent of each other. They came to an understanding with each other, however, before reaching the lake, and forming a junction not far from the southern end of it, they organized the whole expedition under Colonel Ethan Allen, a Vermont officer, who acquired from his bravery on this and on many subsequent occasions great renown.

Capture of Ticonderoga

They sent a detachment to the southern end of the lake—the site of the present town of Whitehall—to procure boats, while the main body proceeded by land through the woods to a point on the shore opposite to Ticonderoga.

When the main body at length arrived at the point opposite the fort, they found that the boats which they had expected from the upper end of the lake had not come down.[1] But they immediately began to make arrangements for crossing the water. They procured all the boats that they could from the vicinity, and engaged a boy named Nathan Beman, who had often gone over to play with the boys in the fort, as their guide.

They waited on the eastern shore till about midnight, hoping that more boats would come, and keeping themselves all carefully concealed. At midnight they began to cross, taking every precaution to preserve the strictest silence, in order to avoid giving any alarm. Those that landed first waited for the boats to return for the others, and when at length it was drawing so near to the morning that they did not dare to postpone the assault any longer—for they wished to break in upon the garrison while they were all asleep—they marched very silently to the entrance of the fort. The sentinel on duty challenged them and snapped his gun at them, but the gun missed fire. The sentinel then fled within the fort, and the whole party pressed in after him, and formed themselves in order of combat in the great square.

The garrison had by this time taken the alarm. They leaped from their bunks and rushed out to the doors, but they saw at once that they were overpowered. They were outnumbered, they perceived, by the intruders, two to one, and they did not attempt to make any resistance.

Colonel Allen went at once to the room occupied by Captain Delaplace, the commander of the fort, and knocked clamorously on the door with the hilt of his sword. Captain Delaplace came in great alarm to open the door to demand what was the matter. His wife,

---

[1] The Whitehall end of the lake is the *lower* end, as it appears *on the map,* it being the southern end; but, as the waters of Lake Champlain have a gentle motion to the northward, and pass off by the Sorel River into the St. Lawrence, the southern end of the lake is really the upper end, and in describing military operations, the terms upper and lower are used in reference to the actual flow of the water, or the descent of the land, and not according to the relations of places to the upper and lower edges of the paper, on which the map is drawn. Young readers very often make serious mistakes by not being aware of this, or by not keeping it in mind.

greatly frightened, came behind him, and stood in her nightdress, peeping over his shoulder.

Colonel Allen answered the captain's question by pointing to his men, and ordering him to surrender the fort. The captain asked by what authority he demanded a surrender. Colonel Allen replied in a thundering tone, that he demanded it by authority of the great Jehovah and the Continental Congress.

This reply has been much admired for the spirit and energy which it displayed; but, unfortunately, it did not express the truth, for the colonel had no authority whatever from the Continental Congress, nor in fact from any other political organization whatever.

This, however, probably made very little difference in the case, in his estimation, as military men, I believe, do not usually hold themselves very strictly to the observance of the rules of truth and veracity, in their communications with the enemy, while engaged in actual hostilities.

However this may be, Captain Delaplace perceived that the case was hopeless, and he decided at once to yield.

Immediately after the surrender was made, Colonel Allen sent all the soldiers in the fort as prisoners of war to Hartford. The military stores which fell into his hands consisted of several hundred pieces of cannon of various kinds—three cartloads of flints—ten tons of bullets—a great quantity of shells—thirty gun carriages—a hundred stand of small arms—ten casks of powder, and about fifty barrels of provisions. All these supplies he sent at once to the headquarters, at Cambridge, of the army besieging Boston.

OTHER SUCCESSES ON THE LAKE

The capture of Ticonderoga was only the beginning, however, of the success of the expedition. A day or two after this, a force proceeded down the lake—that is, to the northward—and took possession of Crown Point, another fort, a few miles beyond, where, as at Ticonderoga, they surprised the garrison and captured the fort without encountering any resistance. Here they obtained another large supply of military stores of various kinds, which were also sent off to the American army before Boston.

After this, the expedition obtained possession of a vessel which they armed, and then proceeded with her down the lake to the outlet of it, where they captured a sloop-of-war, and also another fort which stood on the shores of the river Sorel. In a word, they obtained complete possession of the lake from one extremity of it to the other, and thus enabled the Continental Congress, when it came to take cognizance of the proceedings, to hold under their control the main avenue of communication between the colonies and Canada, besides largely increasing the supply of arms, ammunition, and provisions required for the troops besieging Boston.

BENEDICT ARNOLD

One of the principal and most active of the officers of this expedition, in connection with Colonel Allen, was Benedict Arnold—the officer who afterward acquired so great a notoriety by his treasonable attempt to betray West Point on the Hudson, which had been placed under his command, to the British army.

MEETING OF THE SECOND CONTINENTAL CONGRESS

The capture of Ticonderoga took place on the 10th of May, 1775, on the very day that the second Continental Congress assembled. The first congress, as the reader will doubtless recollect, limited itself in its action to the issuing of petitions, manifestos, and addresses, but the battle of Lexington, and the spirit that it had aroused throughout the country, showed very clearly that the time for parleying was past, and the hour of action had come. The new congress, accordingly, set themselves diligently at work in making arrangements for combining the whole force of all the colonies in a vigorous prosecution of the war.

FINAL APPEAL TO THE GOVERNMENT AND TO THE PEOPLE OF ENGLAND

Before proceeding to this work, however, they made one more final, but most earnest, appeal, first to the government of Great

Britain, by a petition to the king; and secondly, to the people of England, by a memorial addressed directly to *them,* in which they conjured them to come to the rescue of their fellow-citizens in America, who only claimed the same rights and privileges which they themselves enjoyed, disavowing at the same time all intention or wish to separate themselves from the mother country, and only asking that they might continue to live as they had done—faithful and loyal subjects of the king—provided, solely, that they might be permitted to enjoy, as heretofore, the inalienable rights pertaining to them as freeborn Englishmen.

ARRANGEMENT IN RESPECT TO FUNDS

The congress, however, had no hope that these representations could now be of any avail, except, perhaps, to increase the numbers and strengthen the hands of their friends in England, and thus tend to restrain the government, in some degree, in the hostile measures which they were inclined to adopt, and possibly embarrassing them in the prosecution of the war. Accordingly, having agreed upon the forms of these remonstrances, and provided for the issuing of them, Congress proceeded at once to the adoption of the most vigorous measures for carrying on the war.

They voted to issue bills of credit to the amount of three million dollars, to provide the necessary funds, and pledged the faith of all the colonies for the payment of the bills at a future time. The intention was that these bills should be paid out as money for the purchase of arms, ammunition, and supplies, and for the other expenses incurred, and that they would pass from hand to hand among the people as money until the conclusion of the war, when arrangements should be made for redeeming them, by an equitable tax assessed upon the people of all the colonies.

ORGANIZATION OF THE ARMY

Congress next proceeded to organize the army, by combining all the different bodies of men that had so hastily come together before Boston from the neighboring states, into one body, and drawing up a throughout the country an unbounded enthusiasm in favor of a vigorous prosecution of the war. Fresh levies of soldiers were made and were brought rapidly to reinforce the army around Boston; and though the English retained possession of Bunker Hill, they were surrounded and shut in within their lines more closely than ever.

LONG CONTINUANCE OF THE SIEGE OF BOSTON

Things continued substantially in this condition in and around Boston for many months. During this interval there occurred in some of the other colonies several events of considerable importance, which will be more particularly referred to in the next chapter. Some changes, too, took place in the state of things in and around Boston. General Washington took command of the American army early in July, about a fortnight after the battle of Bunker Hill. On the other hand, General Gage was relieved from the command of the British troops in Boston, and General Howe became his successor. The British troops were considerably reinforced and they continued to hold the town, but were not strong enough to issue from their lines and attack the American forces hemming them in.

CONDITION OF THE AMERICAN ARMY

Nor was the American army any better able to undertake offensive operations against them. General Washington found, when he came to examine the condition of his troops, that everything was to be done. There was no order and no discipline. Many of the officers had been elected by the men from among their own number, and knew nothing of military affairs. The men were enlisted only for short periods, and no permanent arrangements for organization and discipline could be made with them. There were no proper arms, and only gunpowder enough at one time to give nine cartridges to each man. There were no tents, not a sufficient supply of food, and no proper means in operation for procuring more. General Washington at once set himself at work to remedy all these evils, but he could only act by securing the adoption of proper measures by the Continental Congress, and in doing this, he could not freely make known his

CHAPTER III
THE DECLARATION OF
INDEPENDENCE

PROGRESS OF PUBLIC OPINION

During the time while the events, related in the last chapter, had been taking place in and around Boston, various collisions and contests had occurred in other parts of the land, the effect of which was greatly to increase and extend the animosity of the people against the government of Great Britain, and gradually to form a public sentiment in favor of sundering entirely the connection which bound the colonies to the mother country, and of establishing an independent nation.

LORD DUNMORE AND VIRGINIA

The people of Virginia were aroused to a high state of excitement by certain proceedings of Lord Dunmore, who was at that time the royal governor of the colony. He began, as General Gage did at Lexington, by attempting to seize a supply of ammunition belonging to the province, which had been deposited in the town of Williamsburg, in an old magazine. Williamsburg was at that time the seat of government for the colony and the residence of the governor.

RESULT OF THE SEIZURE

There was a vessel-of-war, the *Magdalen,* at anchor in the river, a little below the town, and one night, the governor, having made his preparations beforehand, caused the powder to be all secretly conveyed away from the magazine at midnight, and safely stored on board the man-of-war.

The news of the affair spread rapidly on the following day, and created great excitement. The minute men, who had been previously enrolled, as in Massachusetts, were immediately called out, and when a considerable force had been assembled, a delegation was sent to the governor to demand a return of the powder to the provincial authorities.

The governor gave an evasive answer, and some negotiations followed, which were continued for several days—the excitement all the time increasing—until at last news came that Patrick Henry, who lived sixty or seventy miles up the country, was marching toward Williamsburg at the head of a considerable body of armed men, to aid in forcing the governor to return the property.

The governor now began to be alarmed for his own personal safety, and he finally offered to settle the dispute by paying the value of the gunpowder in money. This offer was finally accepted, and the money was paid.

Rapid Progress of the Quarrel

But though the money was paid, the dispute was by no means settled. The governor was a very proud and haughty man, and entertained very lofty ideas of his own importance as a British peer, and as the representative in Virginia of the royal authority; and he was filled with indignation and rage at having been compelled to succumb, in the execution of a trust committed to him by the king, to a mob of low and contemptible provincials. He openly expressed his rage, and in the most unmeasured terms. He issued a proclamation, denouncing "one Patrick Henry and his deluded followers," as seditious and treasonable disturbers of the peace. He threatened, in case any more such proceedings should take place, to make open war upon the province, emancipate the slaves, and arm them against their masters. He turned his own palace at Williamsburg into a sort of fort, established a garrison in it, and surrounded it with cannon.

All these things greatly irritated the people, and made them more earnest than ever in preparing to defend themselves. Public meetings were held in the various counties, and resolutions were passed, in which the character and conduct of Patrick Henry were vindicated in the most decided terms, and committees of vigilance were formed to take measures, in concert with each other, for the public defense.

This state of things continued for several weeks, the excitement against the governor growing deeper, and being more and more boldly expressed all the time. The governor vainly endeavored, by threats and by various attempts at intimidation, to overawe the people and reduce them to obedience. But all was in vain. At length he began to be alarmed for his own safety, and finally he left Williamsburg with his family, went over to Yorktown, and there embarked on board a British man-of-war that was lying there. The name of the vessel was the *Fowey*.

This act of the governor of withdrawing from the capital, which the people of Virginia considered as an abdication of his office, took place in June, 1775, a short time before the battle of Bunker Hill. Lord Dunmore continued for some time after this to send communications to the legislature, and they made respectful replies to them, but at length when the time for closing the session arrived, they reported to him that there were a number of bills awaiting his signature, and requested him to return to the seat of government to sign them, offering to guarantee his personal safety. He refused to return, but called upon the legislature to come to him with the bills, and present them to him for signature at his then present residence—that is, on board the ship. This the assembly refused to do; and they immediately organized a provisional government for the state, through the action of which a series of elections were held, and a new permanent government was organized. The province was thenceforth entirely independent of all control from the crown of Great Britain.

The arrangements for this new government were not, however, entirely completed until May of the following year, about two months before the independence of all the provinces was declared by the Continental Congress, as will presently be explained.

RAVAGES OF GOVERNOR DUNMORE ON THE VIRGINIA COAST

During the interval while the province was gradually organizing its own independent government, Lord Dunmore assembled a naval force in the waters at the mouth of the Chesapeake, and cruising with it along the coast, committed many ravages. He burned Hampton, Norfolk, and many other towns, and sometimes landing a body of troops, he made incursions into the interior, to harass the people, and punish them for their rebellious proceedings. These acts of violence, however, instead of subduing the spirit of the people, only aroused more effectually their determination to resist and defy him. In many of the encounters of his troops with the volunteers that assembled to oppose him, he was defeated. Some of his ships were destroyed by batteries from the shore, and others were driven off the coast. By and by he began to be convinced that his case was hopeless, and at length, after suffering a signal defeat upon an island where he had encamped his troops, and near which he had anchored his ships, the Americans having attacked him by batteries erected on the shore, and destroyed many of his vessels, he embarked on board the remnant of his fleet and went to New York, whence he soon after sailed for England.

RAVAGES OF THE ENGLISH SHIPS IN NARRAGANSETT BAY

The towns on the sea coast of Rhode Island were plundered and destroyed in the same manner, during the summer of 1775, by the British vessels of war cruising there, under the command of Admiral Wallace. The difficulty began by a contest for the possession of the cattle and sheep belonging to the people of the province. There was a rumor that the naval commanders were intending to seize them for the purpose of victualing of the fleet, and a combination was formed among the farmers and their sons, to drive them away into the interior, where they would be secure. This was done secretly, in the night, and Admiral Wallace was greatly incensed at thus losing his expected prize. He immediately began to make demands upon the towns for supplies of provisions, and on their refusing them, he bombarded and burned them. In this way he effected a vast amount of injury upon the people, expelling great numbers of them from their houses, and reducing them to a state of great destitution and suffering.

Barbarity of This Mode of Warfare

Such a mode of warfare as this is universally considered barbarous, and it almost invariably fails of accomplishing its object. Legitimate warfare consists, according to modern usages and laws, in seeking to subdue armed and organized bodies of the enemy, so as to destroy or overcome their military power; and so far as it becomes necessary, in the work of accomplishing this end, to burn towns or destroy private property, there is scarcely any limit to the injuries which may be thus incidentally inflicted upon a non-combatant population. But when the operations of a belligerent have for their direct object and end the destroying of defenseless towns, driving out by fire and sword the unarmed citizens or helpless women and children that inhabit them, merely for the purpose of producing suffering, whether this be done under the influence of resentment and revenge, or as a matter of policy for the purpose of bringing the husbands and fathers in arms to submission, by subjecting them to torture through the sufferings of their wives and children at home, we have a mode of conducting hostilities which is condemned by the common judgment of mankind as wholly unworthy of any civilized power.

These proceedings of Lord Dunmore and of Admiral Wallace were almost as severely censured by Englishmen in the British Parliament as they were by Americans in the provincial assemblies.

The only effect, too, that was produced in the colonies by these cruelties was greatly to increase and strengthen the feeling of hostility to the English government which prevailed throughout the land, and to bring the people more rapidly and more decidedly than ever to the determination to be satisfied with nothing less than absolute independence.

Invasion of Canada

Toward the latter part of the summer of 1775, while the American troops were investing Boston, a plan was formed for sending an expedition into Canada, with a view of taking possession of that province before the British could strengthen themselves there—a plan, the discussion of which brought up very prominently before the minds of the leading men in America the question of independence. On the one hand the English were gathering together their forces in Canada, and might, if undisturbed, before long come down with an army upon the northern and western frontier, and thus attack the colonies in the rear, and in a quarter greatly exposed. It was extremely important to anticipate any movement of this kind. On the other hand, how could the colonies, consistently with the purely defensive policy which they claimed to be pursuing, undertake the sending off of an expedition to invade another province, which made no complaint against the government of the mother country.

BENEDICT ARNOLD

Benedict Arnold was one of the leading projectors of this enterprise. He was unprincipled and vicious, but a very daring and desperate man, and he was at the time making some difficulty in the army at Cambridge by his quarrels with the officers in command of the expedition to Ticonderoga and Crown Point, with whom he had been associated in the operations on Lake Champlain, and with whom he had various disagreements. After much deliberation and debate, it was finally concluded by a committee of Congress which had been sent on to confer with Washington on the subject, to organize an expedition against Canada, and to give Arnold the command of one branch of it. The advance was to be made on two lines—one by Lake Champlain and Montreal, and the other through Maine, up the valley of the Kennebec and thence down the Chaudière, in Canada.[1] Arnold was to take command of the detachment which was to proceed by the latter route.

PROGRESS OF THE EXPEDITION

A large party of carpenters were sent forward to the head of navigation of the Kennebec to build a number of light boats for ascending the river, and soon afterward Arnold commenced his march at the head of eleven hundred men. The troops proceeded by

[1]See map on p. 18.

land to Newburyport, and there embarked on board sailing vessels, which had been provided for them, and sailed to the Kennebec. The vessels took them up the river to the head of navigation, near the town of Gardiner. Here they found the carpenters, who had been industriously at work, and had built them a fleet of two hundred light flat-bottomed boats, such as could be conveyed without great difficulty, by land around waterfalls, and other similar obstructions.

DIFFICULTIES AND HARDSHIPS ENCOUNTERED BY THE EXPEDITION

It would be extremely interesting, if space allowed, to give a full account of the progress of this memorable expedition and of the hardships and sufferings which the men endured—of the severe and exhausting toil required to transport the boats and their cargoes around the falls and rapids—of the difficulty arising from the increasing swiftness of the current as they ascended the river, making it necessary at last for the men to wade in the water more than knee-deep half the time, and pull the boats after them—of the boats becoming leaky and falling out of repair, and of the vexatious delays and the severe labor necessary for rebuilding them—of the spoiling of their provisions from the influx of water—of the discouragement of many of the men, and the consequent, desertions, which were steadily, and not very slowly reducing their number—of the rainstorms and the snowstorms which impeded their progress, and the freshets carrying everything before them which the rains often produced—and of the tangled thickets and deep marshes and frightful ravines, through which they had to make their way in passing across the intervening land between the headwaters of the Kennebec and the Chaudière.

Then in descending the Chaudière, having no guides and no knowledge of the river, they were often caught by the current and borne on resistlessly by it over rapids, and among rocks, and into boiling eddies and whirlpools, by which their boats were often swamped, the cargoes lost, and sometimes the men drowned—and finally, after two months of incessant hardship, exposure, and toil, the little army, diminished in numbers, exhausted in strength, and now very scantily supplied with food and clothing, came out upon the banks of the St. Lawrence, opposite to Quebec, and saw across the river the walls and battlements of the city—the object of all their labors and sufferings—crowning the heights of Abraham, full before them.

FINAL FAILURE OF THE EXPEDITION

The heroism and the fortitude which this little band displayed in their subsequent operations against Quebec, were deserving of success, but they were not destined to meet with it. Arnold's forces were too much enfeebled by the fatigues of the march and by the losses which they had endured, to act effectually against such a city as Quebec, which is built mainly upon a lofty eminence overlooking the river, and was even then so strongly fortified as to make it a citadel rather than a town.

After making some vain attempts to assault the place, Arnold was compelled to await the arrival of Montgomery's army, which was coming by the way of Lake Champlain. When, at length, Montgomery arrived and the junction was effected, operations were commenced in earnest. But they were unsuccessful. The combined force made a desperate assault upon the town in the depth of the winter and in the midst of a violent snowstorm. But the attempt failed. Montgomery, in leading a column of men along a narrow defile under the cliffs, encountered a half-concealed battery, from which there suddenly burst out upon them a storm of grapeshot which swept down great numbers of the men, and drove back the column, and some hours afterward, his lifeless body, with those of many of his comrades, was dug out of the bloody snow. Arnold himself was wounded and disabled, and the troops were withdrawn.

Arnold was not, however, yet discouraged. He remained during the winter in Canada, directing the operations of his force from his sickbed, and vainly seeking an opportunity to retrieve his fortunes. He was obliged, however, at last to give up the attempt, and to make the best of his way back, with the remnant of his army, to the American lines.

Reassembling of the Continental Congress

The Continental Congress, when assembled in the spring of 1776, found that the question of independence was one which they were imperiously called upon to meet and decide. The progress of the contest during the year had only served to widen the breach between the colonies and the mother country, and to render a reunion impossible, and from all parts of the country indications were coming to them that public sentiment was rapidly concentrating itself in favor of entire and final separation. Accordingly, on the 7th of June, Richard Henry Lee, a very prominent member from Virginia, brought forward a resolution, declaring that it was expedient to proclaim the American colonies free and independent states.

The question was made a prominent topic of discussion in Congress for some weeks, during which time also the members held free communication on the subject with their constituents in all parts of the country, so as to ascertain the deliberate and final judgment of the people on the question at issue, and at length, on the 2d of July, 1776, the resolution was passed by an almost unanimous vote.

Course of the Discussion

When Mr. Lee first brought forward the resolution, many of the members were strenuously opposed to it. They thought that by taking such a step, the colonies would alienate from their cause all their friends in England, "who," said they, "if we only remain loyal to the king, and demand simply a redress of our grievances, will sooner or later gain the ascendancy in the government at home and do us justice." On the other hand, any attempt to sunder the connection of the colonies with the mother country altogether, would have the effect, they maintained, of uniting the people of Great Britain against them, and they could not hope to contend alone against the consolidated power of so mighty an empire.

It was replied to this that although alone the colonies could not, perhaps, hope to cope successfully against the power of Great Britain, yet by declaring themselves independent they would be sure to obtain help from other nations, especially from France and Spain;

for they were the natural enemies of England, were extremely jealous of her greatness and power, and would rejoice to assist in sundering her American colonies from her.

There had been, in fact, some negotiations with the French during the year, the result of which confirmed these opinions, for the government had expressed a willingness to give the colonies secret aid, but until the Americans should declare their independence of the mother country, and thus make the quarrel an irreconcilable one, the French were not willing to do anything openly.

The advocates of independence argued consequently that by adopting that measure they could depend upon efficient foreign aid, while in contending for a mere redress of grievances, they would have to fight their battles alone; and that consequently it would be actually easier for them to accomplish their end by taking the highest stand at once, than to aim only at the lower one.

The final decision of the question, however, as is usual in the deliberations of a congress, was not controlled so much by the arguments offered in the debates as by the indications of public sentiment coming in to the members, in various ways, from the public at large. These indications were in this instance so unmistakable, that in the end the resolution was passed, on the second of July, by a vote almost unanimous.

THE DECLARATION

The two following days were spent by Congress in discussing the terms of the great declaration by which the decision to which the community, through their action, had come, was to be announced to the world. A committee had been appointed, some time previous, to make a draft of such a declaration, in order that it might be ready. Thomas Jefferson, who afterward became so prominent a personage in American history, was the chairman of this committee, and made the draft. This, after a few verbal alterations had been made by the committee, was now reported to Congress, and was subjected to a very close and careful scrutiny.

Many alterations and amendments were made to it, and it is now very curious to compare the original draft with the form finally adopted, since the nature of the changes made show very strikingly the calmness and deliberation with which the members acted in this momentous crisis, and the extreme caution and moderation which characterized their proceedings.

NATURE OF THE CORRECTIONS MADE

In the corrections which were made we notice two things that are quite striking—first, a disposition to expunge everything marked by the least appearance of exaggeration in the statements made, or that in any sense represented the conduct of the king of Great Britain toward the colonies as worse than it really had been. For instance, from the clause in the original draft, "He has dissolved representative houses repeatedly *and continually*," the last two words were stricken out. In another place, the words, "He has suffered the administration of justice totally to cease in some of these states, refusing his assent," &c., were softened into "He has obstructed the administration of justice by refusing," &c.; and in another place, the declaration, "He has abdicated government here, withdrawing his governors, and declaring us out of his allegiance and protection," was changed into the more moderate and cautious one, "He has abdicated government here, declaring us out of his protection." In this way everything in the least degree exaggerated or unguarded was struck out, so that there should be nothing left in any of the statements which the declaration contained that was not clearly and indisputably true.

Another striking peculiarity which is to be observed in the changes made, is the expunging of all passages which partook of the nature of declamation or rhetorical flourishing, or appeared to be expressions of excited feeling, such, for example, as passages like the following:

"At this very time, too, they" (the people of England) "are permitting their chief magistrate to send over not only soldiers of our common blood, but foreign mercenaries, to invade and destroy us. These facts have given the last stab to agonizing affection, and manly spirit bids us to renounce forever these unfeeling brethren."

And this:

"We might have been a free and great people together; but a communication of grandeur and freedom, it seems, is beneath their dignity. Be it so, since they will have it. The road to happiness and to glory is open to us too; we will climb it apart from them, and acquiesce in the necessity which denounces our eternal separation."

These and several other clauses conceived in the same style, were omitted, and the simple statement retained, in respect to the people of England:

"They, too, have been deaf to the voice of justice and of consanguinity; we must therefore acquiesce in the necessity which denounces our separation, and hold them, as we hold the rest of mankind, enemies in war, in peace, friends."

In a word, the general object which the congress had in view in the modifications which they made in the first draft of the instrument, was to expunge from it everything that was exaggerated, unguarded, or declamatory in its character, and to send forth to the world only a calm and simple enunciation of facts, and a quiet, though decided and unmistakable statement of the determination to which the colonies had arrived: namely, to take and to maintain henceforth, among the nations of the earth, an independent position.

The declaration thus amended was adopted by Congress by a unanimous vote on the 4th of July.

EXPECTED ANNOUNCEMENT OF THE DECLARATION OF INDEPENDENCE

The sessions of Congress at this time were with closed doors so that no portion of the public were able to witness the proceedings. The general progress however, which the body was making in respect to this measure was known without, and there was a widespread expectation on the morning of the 4th of July, that the business would be concluded on that day. A large concourse of people accordingly assembled in the morning, when Congress convened, and remained hour after hour in front of the statehouse where the meetings were held, waiting somewhat impatiently for the announcement to come forth that independence had been declared, and prepared to welcome the intelligence with long and loud acclamations. The venerable old bellman took his place in the belfry to communicate the news to the town by ringing the bell, the moment the signal should be given; and a boy was stationed below to call out to him when he should receive intelligence from the doorkeeper, that the time had arrived.

THE LIBERTY BELL

The bell that was hung in the cupola of the statehouse where Congress were sitting is somewhat famous in American history, and is considered one of the most interesting relics of the revolution, though now cracked, and no longer serviceable. The curious thing about it is that though cast many years before, it had a motto upon it, which was extremely appropriate to this special occasion. It was customary in those days to cut in the mold from which a bell was to be cast some motto, frequently for church bells a passage of Scripture, which motto would of course appear, when the bell was finished, in raised letters around the bell near the top.

The motto of this bell was:

PROCLAIM LIBERTY THROUGHOUT ALL THE LAND TO ALL THE INHABITANTS THEREOF.

THE PROCLAMATION MADE

The poor bell-ringer, after waiting a long time in vain, became impatient of the delay, and he called out despondingly to the people below in the street "They never will do it! They never will do it!" At length, however, the boy at the door received the proper notice, and he ran out clapping his hands and shouting to the bellman above, "Ring! Ring!"

The bellman immediately began to ring by swinging the ponderous tongue, by means of a rope attached to it, and striking it with all its force against the side of the bell. The people below responded with shouts and acclamations. The bell was very large, being about four feet in diameter at the margin, and it sent the welcome tidings of liberty throughout the city in tones loud and clear. Very soon the discharges of artillery began to be heard, and during all the remainder of the day and night the town was given up to the wildest rejoicings.

The tidings were immediately dispatched by couriers and postmen in all directions throughout the land, and they were received everywhere with unbounded joy. The declaration was read at the heads of the regiments in the army, at the doors of the churches in the country villages, at vast public assemblies in the towns, and was everywhere welcomed with cheers, salvos of artillery, and mutual congratulations offered from man to man; while many banquets, and evening bonfires and illuminations were planned and carried enthusiastically into effect, to give expression to the universal joy.

The several colonies immediately took the necessary steps for forming independent state governments, by which the last remaining threads of British authority pervading the community were all effectually cut off. The necessary changes in the forms of public business, and in official phraseology were made, and everything in a word was brought into harmony with the new position which the country had assumed.

CHAPTER IV
THE CONTEST AT NEW YORK

GOVERNOR TRYON

The governor of New York at this time was William Tryon. He had previously been the royal governor of North Carolina for several years, where he had rendered himself extremely unpopular by his proud, haughty, and domineering behavior, and by the unfeeling severity and even cruelty with which he treated those who incurred the displeasure of the government. He was transferred to New York in 1771, by the British ministry, being deemed a suitable man to carry out with a strong hand in that province the policy of stern and determined severity, by which the rising spirit of disaffection was to be put down.

STATE OF OPINION IN NEW YORK

For some reason or other the British, or, as it was then called, the Tory influence, was much stronger in New York than in most of the other Atlantic cities. This may have been owing in part to the fact that the city, having been first settled by the Dutch, and subsequently taken and held by the British, and having afterwards become a rendezvous of adventurers from various parts of the world, was now occupied by a very heterogeneous population. From its central position, too, it had been, more than any other place, the headquarters of the British forces and the chief naval station; and the town, moreover, contained a great number of naval and military officers, and of civil functionaries of various kinds, who, with the large circle of aristocratic friends which such a class of persons always draws around them, would naturally be conservative, as they called it, that is, in favor of sustaining any existing power.

These persons and those who sympathized with them, managed to gain so great an ascendancy, both in social life, in the city, and also in the provincial assembly, being aided, too, by the powerful influence of the government, that they were enabled for a long time almost entirely to thwart the desires of the mass of the people to cooperate with and aid the other colonies.

Uprising of the People

The governor and his friends succeeded in this policy mainly through the legislative assembly of the colony, which they contrived to keep more or less under their own control; but at length, soon after the news of the battle of Lexington arrived at New York, the people began to adopt vigorous measures for taking the affairs of the colony into their own hands. One of their first steps was to elect members to a provincial assembly, by which the old colonial assembly was very soon superseded. They also appointed, with reference to the management of affairs in the city itself, a committee, consisting of one hundred of the principal citizens, and called it the Committee of Safety. This committee, and those acting in conjunction with it, immediately proceeded to adopt very decided measures. They took possession of the public magazines and arsenals, and distributed the arms and the ammunition which they found there, among the people. They forbade the sailing of various vessels, which the authorities had loaded with provisions to send to General Gage for the use of his troops in Boston. They arrested and imprisoned several of the Tory merchants, who were charged with furnishing the provisions to the government, and finally, with the assistance of some troops which came from Connecticut to aid them, they seized a considerable quantity of arms and munitions of war, belonging to the British army, and sent them to Washington's army at Cambridge.

King Sears

One of the principal leaders in these movements was a very bold and resolute man named Sears, who, in consequence of the great ascendancy which he soon acquired over his compatriots, received the name of King Sears. He was a very energetic and courageous man; and some of the exploits which he and his adherents and followers performed, though they were accomplished by bodies of men very imperfectly organized, were effected with almost military coolness and precision.

REMOVAL OF THE CANNON FROM THE BATTERY

One of the most noted of these exploits was the seizing and removal into the interior of a large number of cannon from the fort and battery. The affair took place late in the summer of 1775. There was a fort, and a battery connected with it, on the point of land which forms the lower end of the city, which had been constructed there for the defense the harbor. These works contained twenty or thirty large guns, and when it became evident to the people of New York, that open war must soon break out there, as it had already done in Massachusetts, the committee of one hundred ordered a certain military company, which was under the command of Captain Lamb, to go and take these cannon, and remove them to a place of security in the interior. Captain Lamb asked for the cooperation of King Sears, and he assembled a large body of the people to go and assist in the work. The time appointed for the assembling of the men was nine o'clock in the evening. The day was the 23d of August.

It had been intended to keep the movement secret, but in some way or other the captain of the *Asia,* a British man-of-war, lying in the harbor, obtained some information respecting it, or at least had some reason to suspect what was going on, and he accordingly ordered an officer to proceed in a boat, with a small number of marines[1] toward the shore, near the battery, and reconnoiter.

When at length these men in the boat saw the company of soldiers, attended by the great crowd of followers, who came to aid them, appear and commence their operations at the fort, some one of them fired upon them. The company of soldiers on the shore immediately returned this shot by a volley, the effect of which was, that a number of the marines and boatmen were killed and others were wounded. The rest made their way back with all speed to the

---

[1]Marines are sea soldiers. There are a certain number of them always on board a man-of-war, to be ready for exigencies of this kind, and also to cooperate in combats at sea. They are armed with muskets. The guns of the ship are worked by the sailors.

Seizure of the cannon.

ship, and the captain of the ship immediately opened fire upon the town, first with two or three single discharges, and afterward with a broadside.

The whole town was instantly thrown into a state of great excitement and alarm. The man-of-war was firing upon the town, no one knew why, or with what design. The bells were rung, drums beat to arms, shouts and outcries were heard on all sides, and everything was tumult and confusion. People believed that the town was to be destroyed, and they rushed into the streets, bringing their choicest valuables with them in hopes to save some portion of their property, or hurrying onward their wives and children, in order to rescue them from the impending danger.

During all this time, the party at the battery went on steadily with their work. They took possession of the guns and removed them to a safe place in the interior, where they were subsequently of no little service in the operations of the colonial army.

FLIGHT OF THE GOVERNOR

The firing upon the town from the man-of-war soon ceased, and the people gradually recovered from their terror, and returned to their homes. No lives were destroyed by the cannonading, but many buildings were injured; and the excitement was so great on the following day, and it continued so to increase, that at length Governor Tryon, fearing new outbreaks, and perhaps apprehending an attack upon himself, personally, left the town, and sought refuge on board one of the ships in the harbor.

He attempted for some time to carry on his government from on board this ship, and he kept up an active correspondence with the leading men of influence in the city, who still adhered to the government, in hopes of concerting some measures with them for recovering the control. But any plans which they may have formed failed of being carried into effect, while in the meantime Mr. Sears wrote to General Washington at Cambridge, urging him to send a force and take military possession of the town.

THE TOWN OCCUPIED BY AMERICAN TROOPS

Washington could not at that time spare any of the troops around Boston, but a plan was soon arranged, under authority from him, for raising a body of troops in Connecticut for this purpose. This plan was soon carried into effect. Governor Trumbull, the governor of Connecticut at that time, entered earnestly into the work, and through his cooperation, and by the vigorous and efficient exertions of Mr. Sears, a body of twelve hundred men was raised and equipped in Connecticut, and put under the command of General Charles Lee. Mr. Sears was made the adjutant-general. These arrangements having been effected, the force commenced its march for New York.

The people of New York were very much alarmed when they found that this force was approaching, from fear that the ships-of-war in the harbor would open fire upon the town and destroy it, rather than allow it to be formally occupied by a military force of the rebels. The committee of one hundred sent out a deputation to General Lee to protest against his coming, saying that Captain Parker of the *Asia* had threatened, that if the people allowed the rebel troops to enter the city, he would burn it down.

General Lee paid no attention to this remonstrance, but continued his march until he reached the immediate environs of the town, and then encamped his troops in what was then called the Fields, but which now is the site of the City Hall Park. He himself went on with his staff into the town, and established his headquarters at the lower end of Broadway. He immediately made a public proclamation, that if the ships in the harbor should be quiet, he would remain so, but that, if they attempted to carry their threat of burning the town into execution, he would seize a hundred of the leading Tories in the place, and chain them together by the neck, and make the first house set on fire by the guns of the ships their funeral pile.

The Tories and Captain Parker knew very well that if the bombardment were to be commenced, the excitement and exasperation of the people would be such that General Lee would be fully sustained by them in keeping his word; and the troops were accordingly allowed to remain in peaceable possession.

Lord Stirling

The second in command—under General Lee—was Lord Stirling, as he was generally called. It may seem strange to the reader that any person invested with such a title should be on the side of the colonies in this struggle. The truth was, Lord Stirling was not an Englishman, but a native of New York, though he had resided for most of his life in New Jersey. His real name was William Alexander. He was of Scotch descent, and he claimed at length, on the decease of certain persons in Scotland, the inheritance of the title and estates pertaining to a Scotch earldom. His claim was disallowed by the English tribunals, but the Americans, believing that he was justly entitled to the succession, gave him the title from courtesy.

The Americans Fortify the Approaches to New York

Almost immediately after General Lee arrived in New York, and took possession of the town, Sir Henry Clinton entered the bay with a squadron, containing a considerable detachment of troops from Boston. General Washington knew of the departure of this expedition, and feared that the destination of it was New York; and that had been one reason why he had so readily entered into the plan of taking military possession of the town by means of troops raised in Connecticut.

General Lee and Lord Stirling now immediately began to adopt vigorous measures for defending the approaches to the town by water, in order to prevent the ships coming up. The squadron did not, however, attempt to pass the Narrows, but after a brief delay in the outer harbor, put to sea again and sailed to the southward. General Lee at once set out to follow them down the coast, with the intention of raising a force and preparing to meet them wherever they might attempt to land.

He left the forces in New York under the command of Lord Stirling, who devoted himself at once, and very vigorously, to the work of completing the fortifications of the harbor. He sent a large body of men one night to Governor's Island, to construct a redoubt;

and another body to a point lower down formed by the westerly termination of Long Island.[1]

In the same manner various other commanding points along the shores were secured, and forts, redoubts and batteries constructed upon them, to compel the withdrawal of the ships already before the town, and to prevent the entrance of others.

ARRIVAL OF GENERAL WASHINGTON

Things remained substantially in this condition until the time of the evacuation of Boston by the troops under Sir William Howe, on the 19th of March, 1776, as narrated in a previous chapter. General Washington supposed that Howe would immediately proceed to New York, and he accordingly set off at once with all the troops that he could take with him, in order to anticipate Sir William's arrival, and if possible prevent his landing.

The urgency of this haste proved however not to be necessary, for it was nearly three months after the evacuation of Boston before the arrival of the British force in New York.

This interval was spent by Washington in strengthening the fortifications in and around New York, in conferring with the Continental Congress in Philadelphia, and in enlisting and assembling troops, and completing the organization of his army.

PLANS AND ARRANGEMENTS OF SIR WILLIAM HOWE

The occasion of the delay was that Sir William Howe, instead of coming directly to New York from Boston, had proceeded in the first instance to Halifax. He had two objects in view in doing this. One was to dispose of the refugee families from Boston, who, it will be recollected, fled in great numbers on board his ships and the transports that accompanied them, when he evacuated the town, where they embarrassed his operations very much, and made it necessary that before attempting anything else, he should make some disposal of them.

---

[1] The situation of the westerly end of Long Island in relation to the entrance to New York Harbor will be seen by the map on page 18.

The other object was to await reinforcements from England, and to organize an expedition anew, on a scale of magnitude sufficient to ensure success in his operations against New York. The accomplishment of both these purposes occupied him until near the end of May.

DIFFICULTIES OF THE BRITISH GOVERNMENT

In the meantime while these events had been occurring in America, the British government, when they found how general and how serious the resistance in America was becoming, and how large a force they were likely to require for the subduing of it, began to be seriously embarrassed for want of men. It has always been somewhat difficult for the British aristocracy, in their government of the empire, to obtain a sufficient number of native troops for all their purposes. The population of the island is not large in proportion to the immense extent of the empire, and so great is the force that is required for so many different and distant operations continually going on, for all the towns and forts that are to be garrisoned, and the losses from disease or from the casualties of the service, which are to be made up, together with the large surplus required on account of the numbers that are all the time waiting in depots, or being conveyed in transports to and fro for vast distances, that it has always been a matter of difficulty to obtain a sufficient number of recruits—a difficulty which is of course greatly increased when, as in the case of a great revolt, there arises a large and unusual demand.

There was another difficulty which the government apprehended, and that was that if they were to raise an army for subduing the colonies, from among the people of England, the men, when they arrived in America and found themselves called upon to fight against their fellow countrymen, whose only crime consisted in claiming for themselves the same rights and privileges which they had always understood were the indefeasible inheritance of every freeborn Englishman, might refuse to engage in such a contest, and even go over in large bodies to the enemy, and make common cause with them, with a view perhaps of settling finally in the new country themselves, and receiving grants of land for their future homes in reward for their services. It was plain that the American government might easily lay this temptation before them, and there was great danger, the government supposed, that many of them might yield to it. They thought it not safe therefore to rely entirely on English soldiers.

THE HESSIANS

In this difficulty the government conceived of the idea of engaging certain German princes to furnish them with bodies of troops from their standing armies, for a consideration in money to be paid to the princes.

Among all the acts of injustice and oppression to which the toiling millions have been subjected in this world, during the last three thousand years, under the despotism of men claiming to reign over them by divine right, it would be difficult to find anything more atrocious than such a bargain as this. That the able-bodied portion of any people should be compelled by the state, or by the prince ruling over it, to arm themselves and risk their lives in military operations necessary to defend the country against an invasion from abroad, or from a causeless insurrection and rebellion at home, we can understand. That they should even be compelled to go beyond the frontier to wage war against a neighboring state, though very hard, may have some plea of justification, when any vital interests of their own land are, or are fancied to be, involved.

But that a prince claiming to hold power over his fellow men by authority from God, should tear away thousands of them from their families and homes, and send them four thousand miles away, to perish from toil, and exposure, and sickness, or to die miserably upon a battlefield, in a quarrel in which neither they nor their country have any interest whatever, merely to put money in their divinely appointed owner's pockets, is so glaringly irreconcilable with all ideas of natural justice, that it seems incredible that such a transaction could have taken place between two of the most Christian and most civilized nations of Europe, and that too, within a hundred years of the present time.

It must be admitted that the proposal, when made, was most earnestly denounced and condemned by many persons in the British Parliament. It was however carried by the votes of the majority. The proposition was made to the German princes and accepted by them. The largest proportion of the troops furnished were from two principalities called Hesse Cassel and Hesse Darmstadt, and from this circumstance the whole body came to be called Hessians. The whole number of German mercenaries thus procured amounted to about eighteen thousand men. They were brought across the ocean by a fleet of transports under convoy of a squadron of men-of-war commanded by Admiral Lord Howe, who was General Sir William Howe's brother. We shall henceforth distinguish these two personages, one a military and the other a naval officer, and who each acted a prominent part in the history of the revolution, as General Howe and Admiral Howe.

General Howe arrived in New York Bay from Halifax, with his Boston troops and the reinforcements which he had obtained at Halifax, at the end of June. He spent a week in reconnoitering, conferring with Governor Tryon, and forming his plans, and then advanced cautiously up the Narrows—the passage leading from the bay to the harbor—and landed his troops upon Staten Island, which forms the western shore of the Narrows—the end of Long Island bounding it on the eastern side.

EXCITEMENT PRODUCED IN AND AROUND THE CITY

Of course the arrival of these immense fleets and armies in the harbor, and the approach of the terrific conflict which they announced, produced a universal commotion. The Tories were secretly exultant, while the timid Americans were ready to despair. Great numbers of families immediately began to pack up their goods and to prepare for flight. Troops came pouring in from the surrounding country, and all was excitement and commotion.

THE MASS OF THE POPULATION STAND FIRM

There were, however, no signs of faltering among the great mass of the population. It was just at that time, as it happened, that the news of the declaration of independence made by the Continental Congress at Philadelphia arrived, and it awakened universal enthusiasm and rejoicing. Copies of the declaration itself were received during the interval between the arrival of General Howe from Halifax and that of Admiral Howe from England. General Washington caused the document to be read to the various portions of his army, drawn up in hollow squares for the purpose, near their several places of encampment. He himself was present at one of these readings, which took place at the Fields, or the Common, as the place was then sometimes called. It is now the City Hall Park.

A few days afterward, a mass meeting of the citizens was held at a public place near what was then the center of the town, to hear the declaration read. It was received by both the soldiers and citizens with enthusiastic acclamations.

All Tokens and Symbols of British Authority Removed

The people, immediately after receiving the declaration of independence, proceeded to remove all the tokens and symbols of British authority from among them—an authority now forever at an end. They took down the British arms from the courtroom, and from the fronts of several public buildings, and destroyed them. They brought out a picture of the king, which hung in the council chamber, and burnt it in the street.

These were, however, all riotous proceedings—the work of unauthorized persons, and wholly unjustifiable. Such objects should have been removed by the order of the proper authorities, in a deliberate and peaceable manner, and carefully preserved, as valuable historical relics, and memorials of times passing away, never more to return.

The Leaden Statue of King George

There was one of the acts, however, of this class that was perpetrated by the populace at this time, which, though irregular and unjustifiable in the manner of its performance, had the excuse of a useful end accomplished to justify it. This act was the taking down of a large equestrian statue of George the Third, which stood in the Bowling Green, at the lower end of Broadway, near the Battery. The statue was to the eye of the observer a golden one, the surface being gilded. But it was really made of lead, and as it was very large, it occurred at once to the patriots, that since the authority of the monarch himself was overthrown, the emblem and image which represented that authority might easily be dispensed with too, and that it would be a good plan to utilize the material of which the statue was composed, by casting it into bullets. The statue was accordingly taken down by a party of citizens and soldiers, in the presence of a large concourse of people, and after being broken to pieces, the separate portions were melted down and converted into ammunition. The statue was so large that the number of bullets cast from it amounted to over forty thousand.

When these bullets came to be used, the British troops, as someone said at the time, had melted majesty fired at them.

However gratifying to the sentiment of poetical justice it may be, that the soldiers sent by a king to reduce his people under his despotic control should have the symbols of their master's former majesty and grandeur, now forfeited and fallen, converted into missiles, and hurled at them in defiance, the proceedings on this occasion were riotous and lawless, and so, wholly unjustifiable. Washington disapproved of them, and having heard that some of the soldiers were engaged in this work, he issued orders strictly prohibiting the men under his command from taking part in any such proceedings in time to come.

First Movement of the Ships

After the troops were landed, and while they were recovering from the fatigue and the privations of the voyage, and the work of making the various changes and reorganizations necessary to prepare them for the new work before them was completed, it was decided to move two of the ships up past the town, and station them in the Hudson River, a few miles above, in order that they might be ready there to cooperate with an expedition which it was expected would soon come down from Canada, by way of Lake Champlain. For as soon as the expedition of Arnold and Montgomery, for the conquest of Canada, as related in the last chapter, had failed, a counter enterprise began to be contemplated in Canada, for sending down a force by way of Lake Champlain and the Hudson River, to meet British troops to be sent up from New York; thus cutting off New England from all the southern states, and dividing the colonial territory in two.

The two vessels selected for this purpose were named the *Rose* and the *Phoenix*. There was some danger in the attempt to send these vessels up, as they would have to pass several batteries which the Americans had erected on the shores. To guard against the shots of these batteries, the decks of the ships were protected with sandbags, and by this means, and by the celerity of their motion, they succeeded in getting by with very little damage.

Besides the hope of hearing of the approach of the Canada expedition from above, and of being able to cooperate with it, there was another motive for this advance. The commanders of the ships were provided with proclamations from the king, and offers of pardon, on submission, to be distributed to the people on the shores of the river, and also with arms, to distribute to such of the population, if they should find any such, as were disposed to join the British army.

The ships came to anchor in Haverstraw Bay, a sheet of water several miles in breadth, formed by the widening of the river. In the middle of this bay they were safe themselves from any missiles which could be sent to them from the shore, but the plan failed entirely in respect to the accomplishment of either of the objects for which the ships were sent—for the expedition from Canada never came down, and the officers found it impossible to communicate with the people on the shores of the river, for the Americans vigilantly guarded the banks, and would not allow any boats to land. Thus the object of the movement failed, but the ships remained above the town.

ADVANCE OF THE TROOPS UPON NEW YORK

In the meantime active preparations were made in the camp at Staten Island for organizing a force to advance upon New

York. The troops could not be taken directly up the harbor to be landed at the town, on account of the batteries which had been constructed to command the approaches; for though two ships of war, carefully protected and kept well over to the opposite shore, might run by these batteries with comparatively little hazard, a fleet of transports—the decks crowded with men—would be exposed to certain destruction, both while passing the batteries, and still more afterward, on approaching the shore, and while attempting to land. It was accordingly determined to land the men on Long Island, below all the batteries, and out of their reach; with a view of enabling them to approach the city by advancing over land, in a line, in order of battle, prepared for a combat on equal terms wherever the enemy might be encountered.

The day on which the landing of the troops commenced was the 22d of August, 1776.

SCENE AT THE LANDING

By referring to the map at the commencement of the second chapter, the reader will see, though on a very small scale, the entrance to New York Harbor, between Staten Island, the small island seen on the western side, and the end of Long Island, on the eastern side, with a dotted line showing the general course of the British army in its advance across the end of Long Island to the town. Of course the southern end of the dotted line shows the place of the landing. Several thousand men were brought across from Staten Island in boats, a very large number having been provided for the purpose. Other thousands were landed from ships and transports. Several men-of-war were stationed near the spot to protect the landing of the troops, by keeping the Americans back, with their guns, if any should appear—for the range of these guns of course extended for a mile or more over the land.

So great was the multitude of men to be moved, and so slow is the process of conveying such numbers with the limited provision of boats it is possible to maneuver in the comparatively narrow space which can be occupied, and so many delays are occasioned by the numerous precautions required, that in this case it was not until the end of three days that the operation was completed. The spectacle was a very imposing one, but there were none but themselves to witness it. A small body of American troops had been stationed on the land near the spot, when the ships approached, but they could do nothing, and were forced to retire. The news, however, of course, spread rapidly to New York and through all the surrounding country, and produced universal excitement and alarm.

PREPARATIONS FOR THE COMBAT

General Washington, who, of course, had not known certainly before by what route the enemy would attempt his advance upon the city, now moved all his available forces across the East River, and massed them at the most convenient points on Long Island, for meeting and opposing the invasion. His troops took possession of the roads and the passes among the hills, and threw up redoubts upon commanding positions, and brought up cannon and supplies of ammunition, and made all other possible preparations for the battle.

The British army, in taking the field after the landing, extended itself in detachments upon a line some miles in length, in order that the several bodies of troops might move forward simultaneously along the different roads, and thus, as it were, present a broad front as they advanced. The disposition of the American troops was similar. Thus marshaled, the two armies drew gradually nearer toward each other.

DEFEAT OF THE AMERICAN ARMY

The grand collision took place on the 27th of August, in a series of skirmishes and battles along the whole line. The Americans were everywhere defeated and driven from the ground. To give in full the details of all the movements and maneuvers, and of the varying fortunes of the day in different parts of the field, would be a long and painful narrative. It is sufficient for our purpose to say, that when night came, General Washington and his brothers in command found that so many of their strong positions had been carried, and so heavy were the losses which they had sustained, that it would be useless for them to renew the struggle on the following day, and that the only hope was of saving what remained of the army by retreating across the East River to New York, and abandoning the whole of Long Island to the enemy.

THE GREAT FOG

If the British officers had known how much the American army had suffered during the day, they would probably have given the leaders no time to consider this question, but would have pressed on upon their whole line by the earliest light of the following morning. But fortunately they did not know, and they were prevented the next day from ascertaining precisely what the state of things was, by a very dense fog which rose from the surrounding waters and enveloped the whole country with so impenetrable a veil that nothing could be seen, and no reconnaissances could be made. It was only in consequence of this fog, as it would seem, that the army was saved; and the Americans devoutly attributed the rising of it to the special interposition of divine providence.

COUNCIL OF WAR

The American officers took advantage of the armistice which the fog and the exhaustion of the British troops, as well as their ignorance of the state of the American army, occasioned, to rest and recruit their men, and to reassemble and rearrange their regiments, scattered and broken by the destructive conflicts of the day before, and also to remove the wounded. While the subordinate officers attended to these duties, the general officers held a council of war, and were unanimously of the opinion, that it would not be prudent to hazard another battle, but that they must retreat immediately across the East River to the New York side. There they might hope to make a stand, and aided by the rapid current of the stream, and by the forts and batteries which they held on the north shore, commanding the ferries and the landings, prevent the enemy from crossing.

This movement they knew very well, if it was to be executed at all, would require to be carried out with the greatest promptness and despatch, and at the same time, with the utmost secrecy. They determined to undertake it the following night.

Retreat of the Army across the River

They, accordingly, maintained during the day as great an appearance of force as possible along their lines, keeping all the regiments in their places except one. This one was a regiment which came from Marblehead, and which consisted of men enlisted there and in other towns along the coast in that vicinity, and who were all perfectly familiar with everything pertaining to boats and the water. These men were divided into small parties and sent down to the river, with orders to search the shores on both sides, and collect all the boats that could be procured, and bring them to certain landings. There they were to wait until night, having each boat properly manned with oarsmen, ready to take the companies of soldiers on board as fast as they should arrive, and row them promptly over.

The Marblehead men did their work well. They collected a large number of boats and held them in readiness. When night came, the men in the camps were all called out and paraded, though, so well had the secret been kept, that no one knew what was going to be done. The several corps were marched down by different roads to the shore, embarked promptly on board the boats, and rowed over.

All this time the camp fires were kept burning, and the pickets regularly on guard at their advanced stations toward the British lines; but when the rest had gone, these men were quietly drawn in and conducted down to the boats; and so secretly had the whole operation been conducted, that none of the British sentinels or watchmen observed anything extraordinary until every man had gone.

Fruitless Pursuit of the British

As soon as the discovery was made, the intelligence was communicated to the commander-in-chief. This was about half past four in the morning. The drums immediately beat to arms, and large bodies of troops were immediately put in motion in pursuit of the fugitives. A troop of horsemen was called out and sent forward with all speed, in hopes to intercept at least some part of the retreating army, but they were too late. As they came galloping down the steep descent which led to the Brooklyn shore, they saw the last boatloads of Americans leaving the land, and before they reached the margin of the water, they were far beyond the range of pistol bullets—the only missiles with which horsemen are usually armed.

The American troops, as they landed on the New York side, did not seek shelter in the town itself, but moved on up the island, following the shore of the East River, so as to be at hand to dispute the passage of the river, if the enemy should attempt to come over, and when they came to a convenient position they encamped. All their movements were in full view of the advancing columns of the British army, on the high lands forming the Brooklyn shore.

ADVANCE OF THE BRITISH MEN-OF-WAR

In evacuating Long Island the Americans were, of course, obliged to abandon the various redoubts and batteries which they had constructed at different points along the shore to prevent the advance of the British ships. The British immediately took possession of these points, and Admiral Howe at once ordered his vessels up to the town. There were batteries on the New York side which interfered in some degree with these movements, but still the ships found it easy to advance up the harbor and to take positions greatly endangering the town. Of course the inhabitants were all in a state of extreme excitement and alarm.

ATTEMPT AT NEGOTIATION

The British fleet and army having gained these immense advantages, and holding now, as they did, the city of New York entirely at their mercy, the commanders determined to pause and open negotiations, in hopes that the Americans would now see that they were overpowered, and would be willing to give up the contest, and spare the further effusion of blood. Admiral Howe, who had been especially instructed by the ministers before he left England, in respect to the terms that he might offer to the people of the colonies, sent a message to the Continental Congress by one of the American generals who had been taken prisoner in the late battles, and whom he paroled for this purpose, proposing to them to appoint a committee to confer with him on the question of peace, and adding that he was empowered by the government to offer very advantageous terms.

This message was a verbal one. The English general would not make any communication in writing for that would have been, as it were, an official recognition of Congress as a legitimate body, with which the British government could consistently negotiate; whereas a verbal message might be sent by a military commander to any organized body of men—to a band of robbers, even, or to the leaders of a mob.

In accordance with this proposal, Congress appointed a committee. The celebrated Benjamin Franklin was placed at the head of it. The conference was held at a private house on Staten Island, nearly opposite to Perth Amboy. The meeting was friendly, and Admiral Howe treated the committee with great consideration and courtesy, though he frankly informed them that he did not acknowledge them as having any official character at all, but considered them as private gentlemen, occupying such positions, however, as to give them great influence over their fellow-countrymen. Franklin replied to this that it was wholly immaterial to them in what light his lordship considered them, but that they really were the official representatives of an independent and sovereign people. Lord Howe replied that he was authorized to offer the people of the colonies very advantageous terms, on condition of their laying down their arms and returning to their allegiance. It was only on those conditions that he was at liberty to make any proposals. The committee replied that it was only on condition that the independence of the country was acknowledged that they were willing to *listen* to any proposals. So the conference was broken up, and nothing was left to either party but to proceed in the vigorous prosecution of the war.

DIFFICULTIES AND DISCOURAGEMENTS

Whatever elements of disorder, or sources of discontent or difficulty may exist in any army, they are always greatly increased, and the evils resulting from them are much aggravated, by ill success; and Washington, when he reassembled his force, after the retreat from Long Island, began to find his situation a very discouraging one. His troops were greatly disorganized by the losses in the battle, and the confusion necessarily attendant on so hurried a retreat. Everybody was discontented and out of humor. The officers quarreled with the men, and the men with the officers; and jealousies and bickerings sprung up between the soldiers of the different regiments, who, coming as they did from different and distant parts of the country, entertained different ideas on many subjects, and were accustomed to different usages; and as is usual with people who have seen little of the world, were intolerant of everything that deviated from their own usual customs and habits of thought.

There were many serious questions, too, to be considered by the officers in command. Should New York be abandoned to the enemy, or should the army attempt to hold it? If abandoned, should it be left to form comfortable quarters during the coming winter for the British troops, or should it be destroyed?

THE BRITISH TAKE POSSESSION OF NEW YORK

These deliberations, however, in respect to the city were soon cut short by the rapid advance of the British forces, and by the demoralized condition of the American army, which rendered it impossible to make any stand against the enemy. Admiral Howe brought up his ships, one after another, to higher and higher points, so as completely to command all the approaches, and also took possession of several islands in the East River, above the town. His brother, the general, soon after landed a force at a place called Kip's Bay, near these islands. There was a considerable American force there to meet him, but they were panic-stricken on seeing the approach of the enemy, and fled from the field in disorder and dismay. Washington himself, who was some miles distant when the alarm was given, galloped to the spot and met the troops hurrying away, their officers vainly attempting to arrest and rally them.

Washington was so overwhelmed with shame for his soldiers at this disgraceful conduct, that for a moment, it is said, he was almost beside himself; and was ready to sink into utter despair. He threw his military hat upon the ground, and was setting off alone to charge the enemy in a fit of frenzy, when the other officers near him seized the bridle of his horse and led him away.

The British troops, of course, made good their landing, and, as this was two or three miles above the town, the American troops that were lower down nearer the town, were in great danger of being surrounded. Orders were sent to them immediately to retreat up the island to Harlem, or across to the Jersey shore. They barely found time to make their escape. As it was, three hundred men were cut off and made prisoners, and several pieces of artillery, as well as a considerable quantity of provisions and military stores fell into the hands of the enemy.

The British troops soon afterward entered the town in triumph, where they were received with great exultation and joy by the Tory portion of the population, which was previously very large, and which now, being joined by all that floating and wavering class, so numerous in every great commercial city, that always adheres to the winning side, became overwhelming.

Having thus gained possession of the harbor and the town of New York, the British troops continued to hold them during the whole period of the war.

CHAPTER V
CAMPAIGN IN THE JERSEYS

The Two Jerseys

When the country between New York and Philadelphia began to be settled, or rather in an early period in the history of its settlement, about a hundred years before the revolutionary war, the territory now constituting the state of New Jersey formed two distinct colonies of the kind called proprietary colonies—the land having been conveyed by separate grants to two different sets of proprietors, in two grand divisions, which were called East and West Jersey. The two together were often designated as the Jerseys.

The proprietary government continued for about twenty-five years, when it was at length abrogated. The two divisions were then united and became a royal colony, under the name of New Jersey. The old designation, however, still continued in use, and thus it happened, that when after the retreat of the Americans from New York, this territory became the scene, for some time, of the most important military operations between the two armies, this portion of the struggle was known at the time, and has been generally designated since in American history, as the Campaign in the Jerseys.

In the course of the campaign, the American army were first driven from post to post across the whole state, from the Hudson to the Delaware. Then, turning upon their pursuers, they soon began to recover the ground, and in the end regained all that they had lost. The principal events of this celebrated retreat and return will form the subject of the present chapter.

The Environs of New York

The reader will observe by a careful inspection of the map, that New York, as existing at that day, occupied the lower end of a long and narrow island, bounded on the west by the Hudson River, and on the southeast by a narrow channel, connecting Long Island Sound with the harbor, which, though really a strait, is called the East River;

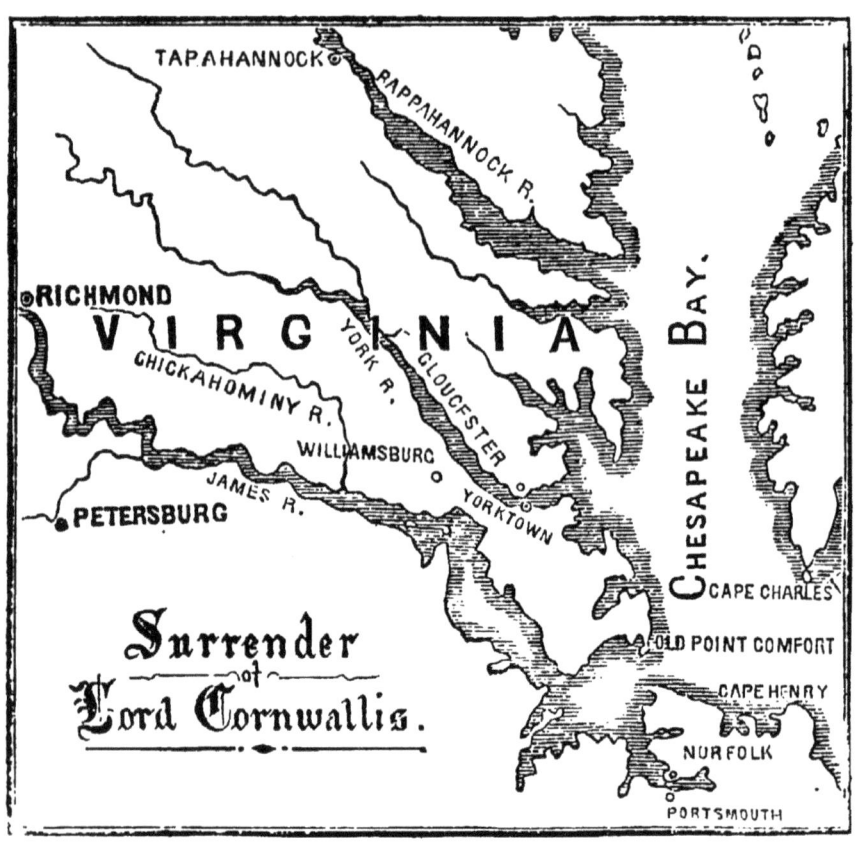

and on the northeast by a stream flowing from the Hudson into East River, where this last opens into the sound. This connecting stream is called Harlem River. It is very narrow, and navigable for only very small vessels.

POSITION OF THE AMERICAN ARMY

When General Washington withdrew his forces from New York to avoid being hemmed in there by the British troops, he moved the troops up to the upper part of the island, near the banks of the Harlem River. There was a strong and somewhat extensive fort, named Fort

Washington, which had been built on very elevated land on the banks of the Hudson, in the upper part of the island, and another fort opposite to it, named Fort Lee. These two forts were the most important strongholds now left in the hands of the Americans—all their redoubts and batteries below having been abandoned to the advancing British army. It was deemed exceedingly important to retain possession of these, on account of the degree of control which they afforded over the navigation of the river.

The American army accordingly, in withdrawing from New York, moved northwardly up the island and took positions on the elevated land in the vicinity of Fort Washington, and on the banks of the Harlem River.

First Movement of General Howe

The first movement made by General Howe, after establishing himself fully in New York, and stationing a sufficient number of troops there to hold the town, was to transport his whole remaining force along the East River and the sound beyond the American camps with a view of taking possession of the whole country there, and extending his lines across from the sound to the Hudson River, so as to cut off the retreat of the Americans in that direction, and eventually, as he hoped, to capture the whole force.

To carry this plan into effect, General Howe caused a fleet of ninety large flat boats to be prepared, and embarking the principal portion of his troops on board of them he caused them to be conveyed up the East River through Hell Gate and along the sound to a point nearly twenty miles from the city, and there landed. Other troops were conveyed thither in transports from the fleet, and a few days afterward a large body of Hessians and other German troops that had just arrived from Europe, were landed near the same spot. This was the second portion of the contingent which the German princes had agreed to send. They were brought over in a fleet of over seventy vessels, and they formed an addition to the force under General Howe's command of over ten thousand men.

The numerous and very complicated operations connected with a military movement such as this—the various preliminary arrangements required, the construction and organization of the fleet of boats, the providing and sending forward of the necessary supplies and the extreme precaution and circumspection necessary in every step taken, make the progress slow. It was at about the middle of September that the British took possession of New York, and it was toward the end of October—nearly six weeks later— before General Howe had effected the landing of all his troops and supplies, and was ready to advance into the interior.

COUNTERACTIVE MOVEMENTS OF WASHINGTON

In the meantime General Washington had by no means been inactive. As soon as General Howe commenced making preparations for his advance, Washington began to move his forces to the northward, in order to thwart his plans, and if he should fail in opposing his landing at least to prevent his advancing into the interior.

The land between the sound and the Hudson River, though elevated on each side, along the water, is depressed in the middle, forming a valley through which the river Bronx flows, as may be seen by the map. Washington, after vainly attempting to prevent Howe from landing and massing his troops, withdrew across the valley to the western side of the Bronx, while Howe remained on the eastern side, beginning at the same time to advance slowly to the northward, in order if possible to get round to the head of Washington's army and intercept his progress.

In order to counteract this movement Washington moved to the northward too, on the western side of the Bronx. These movements, attended by many maneuvers and frequent skirmishes which cannot be here particularly detailed, occupied more than a week, until at length both armies reached the vicinity of the town of White Plains.

THE BATTLE OF WHITE PLAINS

Here the American army made a stand and intrenched themselves in a commanding position, where they were attacked by General Howe on the 28th of October, and a battle ensued known in history as the battle of White Plains.

The battle was without any very decided result, as the Americans in the main held their ground. After a pause however of a few days to wait for certain reinforcements that he was expecting, General Howe made preparations for attacking the American works and carrying them by storm. But on the appointed day a terrible tempest of wind and rain arose, which made it necessary to postpone the attack. Washington took advantage of this delay to escape from the danger which threatened him. In the middle of the second night, just as the storm was beginning to abate, he abandoned his position and moved secretly with all his force to some higher ground farther to the northward, where he intrenched himself as strongly as possible.

This was a narrow escape, for the works at White Plains, though they were made to look formidable as seen by the enemy, were really not much more than a pretense. The ramparts were built chiefly of bundles of cornstalks and straw borrowed from the farmers' barns, and only faced with a thin covering of sod toward the enemy to give them an imposing appearance. They would have easily been knocked to pieces by General Howe's cannon the moment it should be brought to bear upon them.

GENERAL HOWE RETURNS TO THE SOUTHWARD

General Howe, finding that Washington's new position was so strong as to make it inexpedient for him to attack it, gave up the plan of following the Americans any farther into the interior, and immediately began to move to the southward again, toward Fort Washington, which still remained in the hands of the Americans— and was held by a garrison of several thousand men. It was very important to the British to reduce this place, since being directly on the bank of the river, and high above it, its guns had free range over the whole navigable portion of the water, and greatly impeded the motions of the British ships in passing up and down.

RETREAT OF WASHINGTON ACROSS THE HUDSON

Washington, finding that Howe declined to follow him any further to the northward and eastward, and was returning toward the Hudson River, at the point most proper for crossing into New Jersey, concluded that his intention was to move on in that direction, with a view of taking Philadelphia. He accordingly called a council of war, and it was unanimously determined to withdraw with the main body of the army into New Jersey, so as to oppose the progress of the British in that direction.

To effect this movement required some time, on account of the long marches necessary to find crossing places where there was no danger from the British ships, and the delays in procuring a sufficient number of boats. It was, however, at length accomplished, and by the 12th of November the main body were safely over. Two large detachments were, however, left behind—of several thousand men each. One of these bodies of troops was left under the command of General Heath, to hold the Highlands on the Hudson River, and the other, under General Lee, remained near White Plains, to guard the country to the eastward, and prevent any advance of the enemy in that direction.

CAPTURE OF FORT WASHINGTON

General Howe now at once proceeded to make the necessary dispositions for attacking Fort Washington and the various redoubts, batteries, and other outposts connected with it. He moved large bodies of troops into the vicinity of it. He erected redoubts and mounted cannon on the eminences near, and his brother brought up ships-of-war to cooperate with him from the river. When all was ready, he sent in a summons to the commander of the fort to surrender. The commander refused to do so. General Howe then commenced his advance, attacking the works simultaneously on all sides. After a long and severe contest, with varying success in different places at different times, the British were on the whole so far victorious, that they carried all the outposts, took many prisoners, and drove the remaining portion of the American force within the ramparts of the fort itself.

General Howe then sent in another summons to surrender; and the commander of the fort, finding that further resistance would be of no avail, decided to yield. The fort was given up, and what remained of the garrison—two thousand men in all—were taken down to New York, and held there in jails and in other places of confinement as prisoners of war.

Washington, from the other side of the river watched the progress of this contest with his glass, and witnessed at last the proof of the surrender in the subsiding of the American flag and the rising of the British ensign in its place, with a degree of mental distress and anguish almost impossible to conceive.

Extremely Discouraging Prospect for the American Cause

Indeed, the circumstances in which Washington now found himself placed, were in every respect extremely disheartening. His army had dwindled away so much by losses in battle, desertions, prisoners captured in Fort Washington, expirations of the terms of service, and by the considerable detachments that he had been compelled to leave behind him on the east side of the river, that he had now only about two thousand men with him in New Jersey to oppose the advance of his victorious enemy, and to protect Philadelphia and the Continental Congress in session there. The terms of service of his remaining men were rapidly expiring, and the men were so dispirited that they would not reenlist. The officers, too, quarreled among themselves, as is usually the case with the leaders in any cause when things go wrong.

The People Becoming Discouraged

Besides these difficulties connected with the army, strong indications began to appear that the people of the country were becoming discouraged. General Howe issued a proclamation inviting the inhabitants to return to their allegiance, and offering protection for persons and property to all who would come in and take the oath of allegiance to the king. Large numbers of people accepted these offers. For ten days they came in, it was said, at the rate of two hundred a day, to offer their submission. Among these were two or three men who had been prominent leaders in the American cause.

These people, however, gained very little by their hasty surrender. The soldiers of the army, and especially the Hessians, paid slight regard to the "protections" which they received, but ravaged the country and plundered the inhabitants as they advanced, with very little discrimination.

Lord Cornwallis

General Howe was at first somewhat at a loss whether to follow Washington in his retreat toward Philadelphia or to proceed northwardly up the river, in order to cooperate with General Burgoyne, who had organized a powerful expedition in Canada to come down by the way of Lake Champlain and the river Hudson to New York, with a view of thus cutting the territory occupied by the rebellious provinces in two. He finally concluded not to cross the river himself, but to place another officer, Lord Cornwallis, in command of a sufficient force to dispose of Washington's army, and to send him instead, with orders to pursue, and either capture or disperse them, which both supposed would be an easy task.

Lord Cornwallis, accordingly, crossed the river. It was on the 20th of November. He had six thousand men under his command—a number deemed amply sufficient, since Washington had but little over two thousand left, and even this number was rapidly diminishing.

Capture of Fort Lee

The Americans, as soon as they found so large a force coming to attack them, were compelled at once to commence their retreat. It was useless to attempt to hold Fort Lee, the fort on the west side of the river, opposite to Fort Washington, now that the latter had fallen, and the enemy had full command of the river. The place was accordingly abandoned in haste, and all the baggage and military stores which it contained fell into the enemy hands.

Retreat across the Jerseys

The army now commenced that slow and painful retreat across the country toward the Delaware River, which formed perhaps the gloomiest portion of the history of the war. The whole of the remaining part of the month of November was occupied by the weary and dispirited troops in falling back in this way from town to town, undergoing all the time the greatest privations and sufferings, and weighed down by every conceivable discouragement. They moved as slowly as possible, and were obliged studiously to conceal their true condition, and often to turn and present as firm and imposing a front as possible toward the enemy pressing upon them, in order to retard his advance. In this way the weary, wayworn, and exhausted troops fell slowly back, until they reached the Delaware at Trenton, where they crossed the river, the last boatloads leaving the shore just as the van of Cornwallis's army were pressing forward into the town.

The British could not follow, for Washington had taken away all the boats for a long distance up and down the river. The only alternative was to build new boats, or wait for the freezing of the river with a view of marching over on the ice. On account of the time and labor which would be required to construct the large number of boats necessary, and considering also the near approach of the season when the river would be frozen, Cornwallis decided on adopting the latter plan.

MEASURES FOR RECRUITING THE ARMY

Although one might suppose that the work of conducting such a retreat as this would be enough to test to the uttermost the powers of any man, yet Washington, while thus urgently pressed with the duties connected with directing the movements of his army from day to day, sustaining the failing courage of his men, and watching the plans and maneuvers of the enemy, was all the time engaged, in connection with the Continental Congress in session at Philadelphia, in maturing and carrying into effect a most vigorous system of measures for increasing and strengthening his army, and procuring supplies of food, of clothing, and of ammunition, so as to be prepared as soon as possible to turn upon his pursuers, and assume the offensive. In consequence of the arrangements thus made, Washington's army was increased not long after he passed the Delaware, to between five and six thousand men.

SITUATION OF THE BRITISH ARMY

In pursuing the American army across New Jersey, Lord Cornwallis had not followed them up closely with his whole command; but believing, as he did, that the American forces were rapidly diminishing in numbers, and were greatly disheartened and discouraged, he had only sent forward a detachment in advance to pursue them closely, while he followed, marching more slowly with the main body, and leaving considerable portions of his force at the principal towns on the route, so as to hold the whole country securely. Washington, of course, soon ascertained, after he had crossed the river, that this was the situation of the British army; and he learned very soon afterward through his scouts, that there was at Trenton only a detachment, consisting of about fifteen hundred Hessians and a small body of horse under the command of Colonel Rall; and he conceived the bold idea of recrossing the river secretly and suddenly at night, and capturing them.

It seems that Colonel Rall had felt some uneasiness at being so near the enemy with so small a force, and at one time sent to his superior officer to ask for a reinforcement. But the officer sent word back to him that he need not give himself any uneasiness. The enemy, having made his escape across the river into Pennsylvania, would be in no haste to come back again. He would undertake, he said, to keep the peace anywhere on the New Jersey side with a corporal's guard.

A CHRISTMAS SURPRISE

Washington determined to make his contemplated movement on the night of Christmas. He knew that the Germans were accustomed to consider Christmas as a great holiday, and to spend it in feasting and merrymaking during the day, which would be very likely, in the case of soldiers fancying themselves in a state of perfect security, to end in drunken carousals at night, which would bring great numbers of them into a condition very unfavorable for being aroused to meet a sudden irruption of the enemy upon them at midnight, taking them entirely by surprise. So he determined to make arrangements for attacking them at that time.

THE CROSSING

Everything favored the success of the enterprise. The night was dark, cold, and stormy, the air being filled with driving sleet and snow. Washington had arranged his force in several divisions, and sent them to different points along the river, so as to confuse the enemy, by advancing upon his pickets in different directions. The division which Washington commanded in person, was to cross at a sufficient distance above Trenton, to allow of its being completely formed on that side, ready to march upon the town before any alarm should be given. The weather was so cold that the river was full of floating ice, and two of the men, in the course of the night, were actually frozen to death. All these things, though adding, as they did, so much to the immediate difficulty and danger of the enterprise, and testing so severely the courage and fortitude both of officers and men, were extremely favorable in respect to the result, since they aided in rendering complete the sense of security in which their intended victims were lulled.

The boats crossed the river in safety, and the army, after being landed, was formed in order of battle, and marched in two divisions, by two different roads, toward the town.

The darkness of the night, and the quantity of ice floating on the river, had detained the expedition so much, that instead of arriving at midnight it was four o'clock in the morning before the columns reached the town.

ALMOST A DISCOVERY

In the meantime the approach of the American columns, stealthy as it was, came very near being made known to Colonel Rall. It seems that he, as well as his men, was disposed to do special honor to Christmas, and had accepted an invitation to a supper that night with some friends at a certain private house in Trenton. This party spent the whole night in playing cards, feasting, and drinking wine, and were still thus engaged when the American forces began to approach the town. A person living on one of the roads by which they were coming, who was friendly to the British, sent a note by a special messenger to Colonel Rall, in great haste, to give him warning. The messenger, on finding where the colonel was, went to the house, and demanded to see him. The negro servant who attended at the door, said that the colonel was engaged and could not be interrupted. The messenger then gave the servant the note, with earnest injunctions to deliver it immediately. The servant took it in and gave it to the colonel, and he being engrossed in his play, and perhaps somewhat under the influence of the wine which he had been drinking, put it for the moment into his pocket, intending to read it presently. He thought no more of it until the discharges of musketry by the pickets, and the roll of the drums beating to arms, awoke him from his dreamy stupor, and filled him with consternation.

THE SURPRISE

The surprise was complete. No suspicions of the approach of the Americans were excited until they had come upon the pickets stationed at the outskirts of the village. The pickets had immediately fired upon them and then retreated toward the town, giving the alarm. The drums beat to arms, and the whole town was aroused. Colonel Rall rushed out to place himself at the head of his men. The soldiers were hastily formed in the streets, and every possible effort was made to bring them into a condition of defense. But the impetuous assault of the American columns was too much for them. Their artillery was seized before they had time to bring the guns into position, and to complete the climax of their disasters, Colonel Rall, their commander, fell from his horse in the street while energetically attempting to marshal his men, mortally wounded by one of the hundreds of bullets that were whistling through the air.

After this all was hopeless panic and confusion. The body of the fallen colonel was borne away by his aids to a house in the neighborhood, while the men all took to flight, on the road to Princeton, the subordinate officers vainly endeavoring to arrest them. They were, however, suddenly brought up as they were leaving the town by one of the divisions of Washington's army that was coming in by that road. Seeing themselves thus surrounded they threw down their arms and surrendered themselves prisoners of war.

The number thus secured, nearly all Hessians, was about a thousand, including twenty or thirty officers. A considerable number both of men and officers were killed before the surrender. The Americans took moreover six brass cannon, and a thousand stand of arms.

And all this with the loss of only two private soldiers killed, besides the two that perished with the cold.

RETURN OF THE FORCE ACROSS THE RIVER

As it was only a detachment of the British army that were thus captured, and as the main body were not very far distant in the interior, it was necessary for Washington to make immediate arrangements for recrossing the river, with his prisoners and his spoils. He liberated all the officers on their parole. He went to the house where Colonel Rall was lying to pay his dying enemy a visit, and to render him such services of kindness and of sympathy as it was in his power to bestow. He then commenced recrossing the river with his command, and before midnight of the 26th, the whole force, with all the prisoners, and all the property captured, were safe on the Pennsylvania side, and the boats secured there, making it impossible for the enemy to follow.

EFFECT OF THIS VICTORY UPON THE COUNTRY

The news of this victory spread very rapidly and it produced an electric thrill of surprise and pleasure throughout the whole land. The Americans were everywhere greatly animated and encouraged, while the British and their partisans were confounded and amazed. Congress immediately passed acts clothing Washington with new and extraordinary powers. They knew that now, after this exploit, public opinion would sustain them in such a measure. Recruits too began soon to come in, and the men, inspired with fresh confidence and courage were ready to cooperate cordially with him in all his plans and arrangements. Thus in the course of about two days from the victory at Trenton, Washington found himself strong enough to attempt the offensive once more. He crossed the river to Trenton again, and very soon performed another very successful exploit.

THE BATTLE OF PRINCETON

Immediately after the capture of the force at Trenton, the British abandoned all the minor posts which they held along the river, and withdrawing into the interior, concentrated their forces at Princeton. Washington then, after remaining a few days on the Pennsylvania side, and completing his arrangements there, crossed the river again, and took formal possession of Trenton, with a view to retaining it.

Upon this, Lord Cornwallis advanced with the main body of his army, leaving a small force at Princeton, toward Trenton, to attack Washington there. Washington posted himself in a strong position, with a small river—a branch of the Delaware—in his front, and succeeded during the first day in repulsing the British in all their attempts to pass over it. When night came, the operations were suspended, but Lord Cornwallis made preparations to renew his assault in the morning, with a degree of energy which he thought would make him sure of success. He said to one of his officers in the evening, that he was certain to "catch the fox" the next day.

All night they saw the camp-fires of the Americans burning in a long line on the other side of the little stream; but when the morning came, and the daylight enabled him to reconnoiter with his glass, they saw the camp-fires still burning, but not a man nor a tent was anywhere in view. Washington had marched away his whole force during the night, ordering the last men to pile on fresh supplies of fuel upon all the fires, so as to keep up the semblance of an occupied camp as late as possible into the morning.

The question for Lord Cornwallis was now where the fugitives had gone. His first idea was that they had made their escape across the river into Pennsylvania again; but before long the faint and distant booming of cannon was heard in exactly the contrary direction—that is, toward Princeton, where Cornwallis had left what remained of his army; and New Brunswick, where all his stores and supplies of ammunition were deposited, lay a little way beyond. Lord Cornwallis thought at first the sound might be thunder—a mistake excusable enough, since he was an Englishman, and unacquainted with the American climate. No American would think of hearing thunder on a clear, cold, and frosty January morning.

"No," exclaimed one of his brother officers, after listening to the sound, "it is no thunder! To arms! To arms! We are outgeneraled. It is the sound of Washington's guns!"

Cornwallis at once put his troops in motion for Princeton, but arrived only in time to meet the flying remnants of the army that he had left there, and to learn that Washington had taken the place, destroyed, dispersed, or captured the troops, and was then marching off to the northward with his prisoners and his spoils.

MODERATION IN VICTORY

Cornwallis was, moreover, now quite alarmed for the safety of his military stores and his supplies of provisions that were deposited in New Brunswick, which lies beyond Princeton, in the direction in which Washington was moving, and which, of course, were now in great danger of being captured, and either carried away or destroyed. Washington was, indeed, strongly tempted to push on at once, and make an attack upon New Brunswick; but on consulting with his officers, it was concluded that the risk would be too great, as Cornwallis was now rapidly coming up, with a greatly superior force. Besides, his men were now almost entirely exhausted with their late incessant labors and sufferings. They were scantily clothed. Many of them were even barefooted, and were obliged to walk in that way over the snowy and frozen ground. They had had no time for any proper breakfast that morning, nor, if the attempt were to be made to march to New Brunswick, would it be possible to make any halt for the purpose of supplying them with food.

So Washington concluded that it would be better to be satisfied, for the time being, with the advantages which he had already obtained, rather than to risk all, by grasping at more. So he turned off to the left, into a retired road leading to the northward, and then, after crossing a river and destroying the bridge behind him to prevent the enemy from following him, he brought his army to a halt, to allow them some refreshment and repose. The men were so exhausted that numbers of them, as soon as they were at liberty, lay directly down upon the frozen ground wherever they could find a place, and sank immediately into a long and profound slumber.

After allowing the men a few hours of rest, and distributing among them a proper supply of food, Washington resumed his march and proceeded to Morristown, which, as will be seen by the map, lies to the northward of Princeton and New Brunswick. He took possession of some elevated ground in the vicinity of Morristown, and here established an intrenched camp, where he felt that he was safe.

An Unexpected Supply of Warm Clothing

His troops received very soon an addition to their supply of winter clothing in a somewhat unexpected way. When Lord Cornwallis discovered what road the American forces had taken, he made all haste to pursue them. He was stopped by the bridge being down, but he immediately caused it to be repaired, and pressed forward again; and to make up for lost time, he drove the teams which conveyed his baggage and supplies so rapidly over the frozen ground, that many of the wagons became disabled. He collected these wagons together, and left a body of two or three hundred men to guard them while he hurried forward with the rest.

Now there was a company of militia men in that neighborhood consisting, it is said, of only fifteen or twenty men. These men conceived the idea of frightening this guard away from their charge, and capturing the wagons. So they waited until night, and then spreading themselves over a great space among the trees around the spot, they all at once, at a concerted signal, set up an unearthly shout, and began firing into the camp of the guard—advancing upon them at the same time as rapidly as possible. The guard hearing the shouts of the men, and the reports of the guns, coming as it were from all directions, indicating that the enemy occupied a wide front, imagined that they were very numerous. While some attempted to keep back the assailants, the rest hastily put the horses to such of the wagons as they had already repaired and then they commenced a rapid retreat toward New Brunswick, leaving a considerable number of the wagons in the hands of the Americans, by whom they were soon put in order and taken to Washington's camp, where they were found to contain what the troops were most in need of—warm clothing.

ENCAMPMENT AT MORRISTOWN

Washington, on his arrival at Morristown, proceeded at once, as has already been said, to establish a permanent camp there, and in a strong position, where his men, when not engaged in active expeditions, might enjoy some degree of comfort during the remainder of the winter. He established his own headquarters in a tavern, and set the men at work to build log huts for themselves, which furnished them ample shelter. Fuel was quite easily to be obtained from the surrounding woods, and provisions were tolerably plenty. Still the men suffered much for want of comfortable clothing, especially in the numerous expeditions which were made by detachments that were sent off from time to time, to attack particular posts, cut off trains of supplies, and otherwise harass the enemy.

These expeditions were, however, on the whole very successful, so much so that before spring the British army was driven almost entirely out of New Jersey.

INCREASE OF PUBLIC CONFIDENCE IN WASHINGTON

The success of these operations in the Jerseys produced a great effect throughout the nation, and greatly increased the confidence that was felt in Washington, both in Congress, and among the people throughout the country at large. Under these circumstances Congress thought it best to enlarge his powers, and confer upon him a much wider discretion than he had exercised before, so as to enable him to act in a more prompt and vigorous manner than would be possible while he was obliged to wait for their sanction for all important movements and measures, before he could carry them into effect. They conferred upon him extraordinary powers in respect to raising troops, appointing officers to command them, procuring supplies, and making arrangements in all respects for an efficient prosecution of the war. The country at large approved of this policy, and it is now universally admitted that Washington exercised the almost dictatorial powers entrusted to him, with singular prudence and moderation, and without any regard to his own interest and aggrandizement, but solely with a view to the advancement of the cause committed to his hands.

THE MALCONTENTS

Still there was a considerable minority of malcontents and fault-finders. The burden of their complaints was, as it always has been in our history, and probably from the nature of the system of government which it would seem must necessarily prevail on this continent for an indefinite period to come—always will be—the usurpation of state rights. They charged that Congress in conferring these powers on Washington were exceeding their own powers, and were encroaching on the rights of the states, and that their attempt to do so ought to be resisted.

Of course it was chiefly the party of the Tories—friends of British power and the enemies of independence—that took the lead, sometimes openly and sometimes secretly, in encouraging these complaints. It was their mode of opposing the measures of Congress and the operations of Washington, and aiding, without appearing to intend to aid, the cause of the enemy.

This is a difficulty which, in every war in which this country shall ever be engaged, must necessarily arise. The system of policy which has prevailed from the very beginning among this people, during the times of the Continental Congresses, under the articles of confederation, and under the federal constitution, and which will doubtless continue to prevail through the course of all the modifications which the constitution will hereafter undergo, is that in ordinary times, when the country is at peace, and the people are engaged in their avocations of quiet industry, the separate states shall manage their affairs each for itself in its own way, with very little interference from the united will of all. At such times power naturally separates itself and gravitates in portions, each to its own sphere. There is no occasion *then* for the united will to express itself.

But when a foreign war arises—or an extended and dangerous insurrection—or any other crisis threatening the nation as a whole— then the power of the whole, as a whole, will arise and assert itself, and will necessarily interfere more or less, and so far as is necessary to accomplish the ends in view, with the several divisions, in the exercise of powers which in ordinary times they were accustomed to hold in exclusive and unquestioned possession. Then those, who oppose the united will, from whatever motive, will of course at once make the alleged encroachment upon state rights their most available party cry.

The evil was greater in Washington's day than it is now, for then the Congress by whose authority he acted, had in theory no expressed or well-defined powers, but only such vague and uncertain control as public sentiment and the exigencies of the crisis conferred upon them. We have now, however, a written constitution, which distinctly invests the national government with the power of making war, whenever necessary to save the country, either from foreign aggression or from internal violence; and the power to make war carries with it all those extraordinary, and in a great measure irresponsible powers, which by the international laws and usages of the civilized world, are accorded to every belligerent, and before which unfortunately personal rights and civil institutions, when they come into collision with them, must necessarily in some degree give way.

Still, notwithstanding all the authority which any written constitution can give, whenever the national power, long accustomed to lie dormant, is called forth into action, in any great and momentous crisis, those who oppose, for any reason, the end in view, or the general course pursued for the attainment of it, will always make the inevitable, though exceptional and temporary expansion of the national power, and its entrance for certain purposes into what is ordinarily the domain of local law—which is inevitable, though exceptional and temporary—the chief vantage ground of their opposition and their great rallying cry.

Washington found it so. The opposition, however, which he had to encounter in this way, did not daunt him or deter him from the vigorous prosecution of his work, though it greatly increased the difficulties and embarrassments which he had to overcome.

CHAPTER VI
THE EXPEDITION OF BURGOYNE

THE AVENUE TO CANADA

T he reader will perhaps recollect that it was stated in the last chapter that General Howe, after gaining possession of New York, and forcing the American armies to retire—a portion to the northward up the Hudson, and the rest into New Jersey—was at first in doubt which portion he should follow, being for a time strongly inclined to move up the Hudson, with a view of cooperating with a force which it was intended to organize in Canada, to come down through the great valley which separates New England from New York, and which is marked to the eye upon the map by the course of the river Sorel and Lake Champlain toward the north, and by the river Hudson toward the south. This valley forms, as it were, a grand avenue of connection between the Atlantic territory and Canada, and has always been, in time of war, from the very earliest period, the scene of the most important military operations.

The plan of the British government was, to organize in Canada a force large enough to march down and take possession of this whole valley, so as to cut off the New England states entirely from New York and the more southern colonies, thus dividing in two the territory in insurrection, and rendering it impossible for the two portions to act any longer in concert.

GENERAL BURGOYNE

This plan was formed in England by the king in council, and the execution of it was entrusted to General Burgoyne, a nobleman of quite high standing in the English court. Burgoyne had already seen considerable service in America, particularly in wars with the French and Indians some years before, when he had the opportunity to become well acquainted with the country, through which this grand expedition was now to be made. He arrived at Quebec to take command of the enterprise in March, 1777.

The governor of Canada at this time was Sir Guy Carleton. He was disappointed, and felt in some degree humiliated, that the command of this undertaking had not been conferred upon him. He, however, rendered Burgoyne all possible aid in organizing the expedition, and in making all the necessary preparations and arrangements.

The Rendezvous

The place of rendezvous of the expedition was at St. Johns, which stands, as will be seen by the map at the commencement of the second chapter, on the banks of the Sorel, not very far from where that river issues from the lower, that is, the northern end of Lake Champlain. Here the vessels that were required were built, and the stores were collected. By the first of June the preparations were complete, and an army of eight thousand men was assembled. Besides the British troops, there was a considerable force of Germans, and a large number of Canadian boatmen, lumbermen, porters, and other laboring men, necessary to perform the various services required in conducting an army through the forests and along the courses of the half navigable streams, which occupied the country to be traversed, between the headwaters of Lake Champlain and the Hudson River.

Indian Allies

The expedition set sail from St. Johns, and moving up the river in a large fleet of transports and vessels-of-war, entered Lake Champlain, and thence passing on without resistance, through the greater portion of the lake, came at length to the region of Crown Point and Ticonderoga, the first forts held by the Americans. Just before reaching Crown Point, General Burgoyne landed to confer with a large body of Indians, whom he had appointed to meet him there. After the usual feastings and carousings, and the various war dances and other barbarous rites customary among savages on such occasions had been duly celebrated, Burgoyne made an arrangement with the Indians to furnish him four hundred warriors to add to his force. Having secured this accession to his army, he prepared to advance into the region of the American settlements, on the frontiers of which he had now arrived.

A Proclamation

He immediately issued a proclamation, addressed to the people of the country, calling upon them to submit at once, in order to save themselves from the horrors of the war which he was about to wage upon them. The proclamation announced in a somewhat grandiloquent manner the immense and overwhelming superiority of British power, and the hopelessness of any attempt on their part to resist it. Besides this, he informed them of the large Indian force that was joined with him, reminded them of the savage atrocities which these barbarians were accustomed to commit, and which it would be wholly impossible for him to restrain. By these and similar representations he endeavored to overawe the population of the country, and induce them to submit at once to the restoration of the British authority over them.

Excitement and Alarm among the Americans

In the meantime all was excitement and alarm among the Americans. The plan of this invasion had been kept in a great measure secret, and Congress had made no adequate preparations to meet it. The people, too, in all the region of country through which the army of the invaders was about to advance, were especially alarmed. They began to make hurried preparations for defense. Troops were raised and marched to and fro. The country was filled with wild reports and rumors, and various and conflicting opinions were formed in respect to what ought to be done. There were personal differences, too, among the officers in command of the forces in that part of the country, arising from rivalries and mutual jealousies. The two principal generals were Gates and Schuyler. There was quite a contention to determine which of them should be placed in chief command of the army to meet Burgoyne. After much debate and difficulty, Congress appointed Schuyler. Then Gates took offense and refused to serve under Schuyler, or to render any cooperation. Thus, on the part of the Americans, all was excitement, and alarm, and disputing, and confusion.

CAPTURE OF THE LAKE CHAMPLAIN FORTS

Under these circumstances it was not to be expected that Burgoyne should at first meet with any serious resistance, and in fact he did not. For a time, his army advanced victoriously, carrying everything before it. The first point of attack was the fort at Ticonderoga. Burgoyne landed his forces and his artillery a short distance north of the fort, and began to take positions on the hills surrounding and commanding it; but General St. Clair, the American officer, in authority, did not wait for the attack. He had previously placed a strong boom across the lake, at the fort, which, together with a bridge which was built here, formed obstructions that effectually prevented the British squadron from advancing beyond that point until the fort was taken. His own vessels—those that remained of the American fleet on the lake—were above, that is, to the southward of the obstruction.

He at once embarked a portion of his men on board these vessels, very secretly at night, and put all the ammunition and military stores which he could remove from the fort on board a number of large, flat-bottomed boats, and then abandoning the fort, he made the best of his way southward to the upper end of the lake, and landed his flotilla there, at the place where the town of Whitehall now stands.

The rest of the men were moved in profound silence over the long bridge which crossed the lake at this point, and thence commenced their march by land, through the woods, to the southward.

This escape was effected with great difficulty. In fact it came very near being defeated altogether, for the British army had possession of heights on the shore that commanded a full view of the water; and it was only by making the arrangements in the most secret manner possible, and accomplishing the whole movement in the dead of night, that the retreat could be effected at all. As it was, it was discovered somewhat prematurely, by the light of a building that was set on fire on the other side of the lake, just as the last of the men were retiring, and the British immediately commenced measures for a vigorous pursuit.

Of course on the evacuation of Ticonderoga, all the other forts and strongholds of the Americans on Lake Champlain were abandoned too, and the whole fell together into Burgoyne's hands.

PURSUIT OF THE AMERICANS

There were two detachments sent in pursuit of the Americans. One consisted of a squadron of vessels sent up the lake, as soon as the boom and the bridge could be broken through, to intercept the flotilla which conveyed the stores and ammunition to what is now Whitehall, and the other a force by land, to follow the army. Both were successful. The convoy of the stores was overtaken, and the stores were all captured and conveyed back to the fort; and the rear-guard of the retreating army was also intercepted, a few miles from Castleton,[1] in Vermont, on their way to the southward. They were attacked and defeated with great loss, and some hundreds were made prisoners.

A few succeeded in making their escape to the main body, some miles farther on, and the whole then continued to retreat rapidly to the southward, in order to meet and join the forces of General Schuyler, who had now organized his army, and was coming up the Hudson.

CONTINUED RETREAT OF THE AMERICANS

The reader will observe by the map, that between the upper, that is, the southern end of Lake Champlain, and the nearest waters of the Hudson, there is a tract of land to be passed, which, as may be seen by comparing it with the scale of miles, is about twenty-five miles in extent. This was a famous portage in those days, and was much traveled by means of a rough road constructed through the woods, with long causeways of logs over the swampy portions of the ground, and rude bridges for crossing the small streams. This road

---

[1]See map on p. 18.

Obstructing the way.

was guarded by three forts: one, Fort Skene, at the upper extremity of the road, where Whitehall now stands; another, Fort Anne, midway, and a third, Fort Edward, at the end of it, on the Hudson—not, however, where the waters of the Hudson are first reached, but some miles below, where the river first begins to be navigable. This lower fort, Fort Edward, was the place appointed by General Schuyler as the rendezvous of his forces, both of those who were retreating from the lake, and of those who were assembling from the neighboring states, or coming up the Hudson, to form the new army.

To this point, accordingly, the broken and defeated columns that Burgoyne was pursuing endeavored to make their way by the road above described. As they advanced, they halted here and there, to obstruct the passage as much as possible, in order to retard their enemies in their pursuit. They filled the channel of a creek, which might be used for boats, at a certain part of the way, with impediments to navigation; they broke up the causeways; they burned or demolished the bridges, and at every narrow pass they closed up the road with trees, which they felled into it, from the sides, in such a manner as that the branches, inextricably intertwined together, should effectually bar the way, and also require a great deal of time and a vast amount of labor for the removal of them.

Thus the scattered remains of the American troops moved on until they reached Fort Anne, the middle station of the portage. Here they at first thought that they should be able to make a stand, but finding that the enemy were coming on in overwhelming force, they set fire to the fort and all the buildings connected with it, and then resumed their retreat, still continuing to break up and obstruct the road behind them, in order to impede as much as possible their enemies in the pursuit.

Excitement in Congress and throughout the Country

As the news of these events reached Congress and spread through the country, they awakened a general indignation, as well as universal alarm. The generals in command were considered to have evinced great cowardice or great incompetency, in allowing themselves to be so easily expelled from positions so strong, with so large a force, too, under their command. Many of them were, for a time, denounced as traitors, and charged with acting in collusion with the enemy. But on a calm investigation of the whole case, which took place subsequently, it was proved to the satisfaction of Congress and the country, that under the circumstances in which they were placed, they could not have acted otherwise than they did; and they were finally exonerated from all blame.

BRIEF OCCUPATION OF FORT EDWARD

At length the retreating troops reached Fort Edward, and were joined there by the army of Schuyler, which had come up the river, and by other bodies of troops assembling there from all the neighboring region. Fort Edward was a very strong and capacious work, the walls surrounding it being sixteen feet high and twenty feet thick, and built of logs and earth.

Schuyler established himself at this post, but he did not long remain here. Burgoyne was steadily advancing, and though his progress was very slow on account of the delay which the impediments and obstructions in the road occasioned him, he at length arrived safely on the banks of the Hudson, where the way was comparatively open before him to Fort Edward. Schuyler did not consider himself yet strong enough to make a stand against the British force, and so he evacuated the fort and moved down the river to the mouth of the Mohawk, where he made another stand.

EXPEDITION INTO VERMONT

These various movements and operations had occupied so much time, that it was now the first of August. Burgoyne had been delayed, moreover, in some degree, by his desire to open communications with the people of the country, large numbers of whom were opposed to the independence of the colonies, and many of them were ready to join his army. He did, in fact, in this way receive large accessions to his force. And now he conceived the idea of sending out an expedition into the borders of Vermont, to procure more aid of this character.

He gave the command of the expedition to Colonel Baum, and the object of it was, as he said in the instructions which he gave him, "to try the affections of the country, to procure a number of horses for mounting a corps of dragoons, to obtain royalist recruits, and to collect supplies of cattle and provisions."

These last were becoming, in fact, quite essential to him, for the distance from Canada was now so great, and the land carriage for a portion of the way so laborious and slow, that his stock of provisions was nearly exhausted.

The general was destined, however, to be greatly disappointed in the fruits of this expedition, for the fortune of war was now about to turn in favor of the American cause.

PREPARATIONS IN VERMONT AND NEW HAMPSHIRE

During all this time, while Burgoyne had been advancing with his force, great excitement and alarm had prevailed throughout Vermont and New Hampshire, for no one knew certainly what the object of his expedition was to be. There was no special reason for believing that he was intending to proceed down the Hudson to New York. He might, for aught that appeared, be designing to march eastward into New England, and to Boston. There was consequently in all that region great alarm.

The legislature of New Hampshire had accordingly at once determined to raise a force to defend their state; and they put the men under the command of General Stark, a plain farmer of the interior, who had, however, seen considerable service already, and had distinguished himself by a sort of blunt sagacity and a cool and quiet, but determined energy, which gave him great influence over his men. The rustic and almost homely simplicity of his character is shown by what he said to his soldiers, as they were going into battle, when they at length met the enemy, in lieu of the pretentious and grandiloquent speech often made by commanders on such occasions. The men were ascending a piece of rising ground, led by him, when they suddenly came in sight of the long lines of British troops in the celebrated scarlet uniforms, of which his men had often heard, but which many of them had never yet seen.

"There, boys!" said he; "there are the red coats! We will either have them all in our hands before night, or Molly Stark's a widow."

He was not at this time, unfortunately, on good terms with Congress, however, having taken offense at some of their proceedings in respect to him, and he would not now take command of the New Hampshire force, except on condition that he was to act independently, under the orders of the New Hampshire legislature, and was not to be subject to General Schuyler or to Congress in anyway.

Conflict between the Congressional and State Authority

It was in consequence of this special arrangement made between the legislature of New Hampshire and General Stark, that there arose what was perhaps the first decided case of collision between the authority of the general government of the country and that of a particular state, of which afterward so many instances occurred, and which led to such serious embarrassments. Congress had appointed General Schuyler to command all the forces which might be raised in any of the states within this, the northern, department. New Hampshire, on the other hand, had appointed General Stark to lead the forces of that state, and had given him an independent command of them.

General Schuyler sent an officer to meet Stark as he was advancing, with an order that he should come immediately with his troops to Fort Edward, and there join the main body. Stark refused to obey this order, and to sustain himself in his refusal produced the instructions which he had received from the authorities of the state of New Hampshire. Schuyler then reported the facts to Congress, and Congress passed a vote of censure on the legislature of New Hampshire. The whole affair led to a great deal of difficulty, and would probably have led to much more, had not the signal victory which General Stark soon obtained at Bennington turned all thoughts into other channels, and changed the spirit of bickering and complaint into a universal sentiment of triumph and joy.

THE BATTLE OF BENNINGTON

Colonel Baum at the head of his detachment, consisting of British and German troops, and of a large number of royalists from the country, who had joined him, together with a considerable body of Indians, crossed the frontier of Vermont, and advanced without any opposition as far as to Bennington. Here, finding that Stark was now close at hand with his New Hampshire troops and a body of "Vermont boys" who had joined him, he halted and encamped on a piece of rising ground near the town.

The American army slowly and cautiously approached. For two or three days there was a pause, which was spent by both sides in reconnoitering, and making arrangements for the coming battle. During a part of this time a powerful rain fell, which also tended to prevent very active operations. At length, however, on the 16th of August General Stark advanced to the attack. A long and desperate battle was fought, the result of which was the total defeat and dispersion of the British forces. Colonel Baum was mortally wounded, and died a few days afterward. Two hundred of his men were killed, and seven hundred were taken prisoners. The rest abandoned the ground and fled at last with such precipitancy as to leave behind them several pieces of cannon, a considerable quantity of arms, drums, and other articles thrown away in their flight, and several wagons of ammunition.

The Americans lost only about one hundred men. About a hundred more were wounded. General Stark was unhurt though he had a horse shot under him.

CHANGE IN THE FORTUNE OF WAR

This battle of Bennington, like that of Trenton in the campaign in the Jerseys, was the commencement of a new era in the operations connected with Burgoyne's invasion. The news of it sent a thrill of joy throughout the whole country, and nerved the people everywhere to fresh exertion. A very few days after it occurred it was followed by another success on the other side of Burgoyne's line of march, that is on the New York side. The success in this latter case was accomplished by a very ingenious stratagem.

Fort Schuyler

Fort Schuyler was situated at the headwaters of the Mohawk River where the town of Rome now stands. It was near the frontier of the American settlements and formed a very important outpost. A considerable force, comprising a large body of Indians, had come down in that direction from Canada, by way of Oneida Lake, with the intention of capturing the fort, and then sweeping down in triumph through the valley of the Mohawk to join Burgoyne's victorious army on the Hudson. They invested the fort, and after various maneuvers and operations on the part both of the besiegers and of the garrison, which extended through several weeks, and comprised some very bloody battles but which cannot here be described in detail, the garrison was at last reduced to great extremity. The men were exhausted with fatigue, the provisions were spent, and the ammunition was nearly exhausted.

Summons to Surrender

The British general sent in a demand for the surrender of the fort, by one of his officers under a flag of truce. This officer, in delivering his message made statements that were entirely false in respect to the progress which Burgoyne had made, and said moreover that they had a large body of Indians under them, who could with difficulty be restrained as it was, and that if the garrison resisted any longer the Indians would, in the end, on finally taking the place, massacre the whole of them, and then sweep through the country with fire and sword, and create universal desolation.

To this the officers replied very indignantly that such a message as that, threatening massacre for themselves and for their wives and children as a means of compelling them to surrender a military post, was one that was unworthy of any British officer to send, and they were surprised that any British officer could be found to bring it; and that rather than to deliver the fort to so merciless and bloodthirsty a crew as the communication which they had made proved them to be, they would run the risk of being tortured to death, by the Indians, in their usual manner—which was by a process of cruelty too horrible to be described.

Messengers Sent to General Schuyler

While the garrison were in this strait two of the officers volunteered to attempt to pass through the lines of the enemy in the night and make their way to General Schuyler's camp. The names of the officers who undertook this extremely hazardous enterprise were Colonel Willet and Lieutenant Stockwell.

They crept secretly out of the fort by the sally port, one very dark and stormy night about ten o'clock. They were each armed with a spear. They crept along upon their hands and knees to avoid the observation of the sentinels, through a morass, till they came to the river. They crossed the river on a log. After reaching the opposite bank they plunged into a dark and tangled wood, the rain still coming down all the time in torrents. They had no means of guiding themselves and so they soon lost their way. At one time they were very near coming upon an Indian camp, but were warned of their danger by the barking of a dog. Finally they concluded to stop and remain where they were until morning.

The clouds broke away about daylight, and some stars appeared by means of which the adventurers discovered the points of the compass and so resumed their journey. They took every precaution as they went on, to avoid leaving any traces of their march, for fear that the Indians might attempt to follow the trail. Sometimes they walked some distance in the bed of a brook, and often returned for a certain space on their track, in order to mislead pursuers. At length after a great variety of adventures, and some very narrow escapes, they obtained horses on the morning of the second day and thence went on rapidly until they reached General Schuyler's camp in safety.

Arnold's Ruse

This was before the success at Bennington, and Schuyler and his officers were much at a loss, and greatly divided in opinion, as to what it was best to do. Finally, it was determined to send a body of men to relieve the fort, if possible, and General Arnold, who was always ready when any desperate enterprise was to be undertaken, volunteered to command it. He set out upon his march, but when he began to draw near to the fort, he found that his force was altogether too small to attack the besiegers with any hope of success. So he undertook to frighten them away by a very singular and cunningly contrived stratagem.

HON-YOST

He had among several royalist prisoners in his camp, a coarse, half-idiotic man, named Hon-Yost Schuyler. He caused this man to be tried by court-martial, on charge of treasonable aid afforded to the enemy, and condemned to death. His mother, who lived in the neighborhood, came in great distress to beg for her poor boy's life. For a time Arnold was inexorable, but at last he consented to spare his life on condition that he would go forward to the camp of the besiegers, before Fort Schuyler, and there, pretending to have escaped from General Arnold, make such representations to the British general and to the Indians, in respect to the force which Arnold was bringing on to relieve the fort, as to alarm them all, and induce them to abandon the siege; and in the meantime, as security for his fidelity, he was to leave his brother in his place, to be shot in his stead, unless he either succeeded in his undertaking, or else returned and gave himself up again.

His mother offered to remain herself in his place, as security for his return, but Arnold preferred the brother. The mother, in fact, would have been no security at all, as both she herself and her son would know that Arnold could not order the mother to be shot, however faithless her son might have proved.

The plan, however, perfectly succeeded. Hon-Yost, accompanied by an Indian, proceeded to the British camp before Fort Schuyler. He appeared first at the Indian portion of the camp, where he came running in, breathless and greatly excited, and showing holes in his coat and clothes which he pretended had been made by bullets in the battle from which he had barely escaped with his life; and he gave such exaggerated accounts of the immense numbers of Arnold's army as to terrify the Indians exceedingly. They resolved at once to retreat, and when they made known their determination to the British commander, he sent for Hon-Yost, and was himself alarmed in the same manner, by the same tales. So he raised the siege and set off at once, in the night, on his retreat back to Canada. His Indian allies nearly all abandoned him, and scattered themselves in the surrounding woods, and the royalists who had joined his standard deserted him and returned to their homes, while all who had been inclined to take sides with the British throughout the whole valley, suddenly abandoned all thought of doing so, and either became peaceable and silent or else began to espouse the American cause.

General Burgoyne's Difficulties Become Serious

General Burgoyne now soon began to find that his situation was becoming exceedingly difficult and dangerous. The defeat at Bennington disappointed him in his expectation of receiving supplies of food from Vermont, and the reinforcements which he had expected by the way of Fort Schuyler were cut off and driven back. His Indian auxiliaries had nearly all abandoned him. His own troops were greatly diminished by the fatigues, exposures and conflicts of the long summer campaign. These causes, which conspired to discourage him and his army, had operated greatly to encourage and inspirit the Americans. The whole country was aroused. Recruits and volunteers came in rapidly in larger or smaller parties, to swell the American force, and to aid in surrounding him. Detachments were sent to the northward to break up the roads leading from Lake Champlain, in order to prevent his receiving anymore supplies from Canada, and even some of the forts and other posts on the shores of the lake were recaptured.

Thus he found himself in the midst of an enemy's country, cut off from supplies of food and ammunition, with a large and powerful army before him and an excited population everywhere rushing to arms, and gathering on every side to surround him and cut off his retreat.

Jenny M'Crea

The plan of bringing Indians with him as auxiliaries might have operated advantageously in intimidating the people of the country and making them more ready to submit, if the expedition had been successful; but as it was, the effect was extremely unfavorable, inasmuch as it only operated to exasperate the Americans in every part of the country, and to arouse a universal and most determined resentment among them. This resentment was greatly aggravated throughout the whole country by the stories which were circulated in respect to poor Jenny McCrea, who was murdered and scalped by the Indians.

Jenny was an orphan. She was born near New York, but had been for some time living with her brother, on the Hudson River, in the vicinity of Fort Edward. She was engaged to be married to a young man named David Jones, who, when the war broke out, took the British side, and went to Canada with one of her brothers, where he interested himself in enlisting men to fight against the Americans, and was made a lieutenant in one of the companies he helped to raise. He joined Burgoyne's expedition, and came down with him to the Hudson.

When the British began to draw near to Fort Edward, Jenny was on a visit up the river a little way, at the house of a Mrs. Neil, where she was very intimate. Her brother repeatedly sent for her to come home to his house, in order to be ready to escape with him down the river; but she knew that her lover was coming with the advancing army, and her sympathies were naturally on that side too. Mrs. Neil was also of that party, and so she continued to remain in her house. At last, when Burgoyne's army began to approach very near, her brother sent her a peremptory summons to come to his house immediately, and he made arrangements to have her conveyed in a boat down the river.

THE CAPTURE

But just as she was about to embark in the boat, a boy saw some Indians coming stealthily toward the house. He ran to the fort to give the alarm, but before any help could come, the Indians had entered the house, and the mischief was done.

The only persons in the house were Mrs. Neil, Jenny, a black servant girl, and two small children. These all, as soon as they heard that the Indians were coming tried to get down through a trapdoor into a cellar to hide themselves. They all succeeded in doing this except Mrs. Neil, who was advanced in years and very fleshy, and the Indians seized her just as she was passing through the door. They also went down into the collar, and found Jenny, and brought her up; but as the place was dark, they did not see the face of the black girl, and so did not find either her or the two children, whom she concealed behind her clothes.

They immediately made off with their two captives, the soldiers from the fort, who had now taken the alarm, pursuing and firing at them. The Indians, however, made good their escape. A portion of them arrived at the camp, bringing with them Mrs. Neil, breathless, exhausted, and half dead with terror and fatigue, and almost naked, too, as the Indians had plundered her of nearly all her clothing. Soon afterwards the others came, bringing with them the scalp of poor Jenny, which Mrs. Neil—overwhelmed with horror—at once recognized by the long and glossy tresses of the hair.

ACCOUNT GIVEN BY THE INDIANS

The story of the Indians was, that Jenny was killed by one of the bullets shot after them by the pursuers from the fort, and that, as they could not then bring her in as a living prisoner, they did what they considered the next best thing, by taking her scalp as a trophy.

We have not space to describe in full the remaining incidents of this dreadful affair—the excitement which it produced in the camp, the anguish and despair into which Mrs. Neil was plunged— the distressing difficulty of her situation, from the fact that for some time no apparel could be found that she could wear—and of her being covered with a military cloak until other arrangements could be made—of the search for and recovery of poor Jenny's body, and its being borne down the river to her brother in the same boat by which she was herself to have been conveyed—and of the overwhelming and long-protracted anguish of Jenny's lover, who never recovered from the dreadful shock which he had received.

EFFECTS PRODUCED BY THE DEATH OF POOR JENNY

The story of this murder went all over the country, and produced everywhere a very deep and profound sensation. It was told in various forms, one of which, and the one which has remained widely current to this day, was, that Lieutenant Jones employed the Indians himself, to procure his intended bride, and bring her from out of the American lines into the British camp, where she could be under his protection, promising them a large reward if they would procure her and deliver her to him in safety—and that, the Indians falling into a quarrel about her, or about the reward, on the way, killed her, and then took off her scalp. This story was very widely circulated, and many other circumstances were related and generally believed, which had no foundation in fact. The particulars of the case were, however, after all, immaterial. A universal feeling of indignation was aroused throughout the country, and even in Europe, at the outrageous atrocity of a Christian and civilized people bringing down with them in a war against their own fellow countrymen and kindred, hordes of such reckless and bloodthirsty savages as these were shown to be, by any of the various versions of the story of Jenny McCrea, which were circulated through the world.

Poor Jenny McCrea! Although her sympathies, through her maidenly love for her betrothed, and her natural interest in the cause which he had espoused, may have been altogether against the American cause, there was perhaps no one life sacrificed through the whole struggle which exerted a more effectual influence on the final and successful termination of it than that of this unhappy maiden.

CHAPTER VII
THE SURRENDER OF BURGOYNE

The Crisis Approaching

Soon after the middle of September, General Burgoyne began to find that his situation was becoming extremely critical. His Indian allies had nearly all deserted him, and returned to their native forests. His own troops had been greatly diminished. The recruiting of his forces from the royalists of the country, on which he had placed great reliance, had entirely ceased. On the other hand, the forces of the Americans were very rapidly increasing—the current of feeling throughout the whole region having been turned altogether against Burgoyne by the reverses which he had met with, the discouraging prospects before him, and by the general exasperation which had been produced by the conduct of his savage allies.

He was for a time greatly at a loss to know what to do. The way of retreat across the land to Lake Champlain and down the lake had already been cut off, and was in the hands of his enemies. Before him, too, the passage was closed by a large and increasing force, and a net was gradually being drawn around him, from which the difficulty of extricating himself was growing greater and greater every day. He at length concluded that desperate as was the alternative, the only hope for him was in the attempt to cut his way through the army before him, and force a passage down the river.

The Battle of Bemis's Heights

Burgoyne accordingly moved onward and crossed the Hudson by a ford below Fort Edward, in order to attack the American army, which was encamped upon certain rising grounds near the river, called Bemis's Heights. General Gates was in command of this army at this time, General Schuyler having been superseded on account of the dissatisfaction which was felt in Congress and throughout the country with his want of success in withstanding Burgoyne's advance in the early part of the campaign, though he was afterwards entirely exonerated from all blame. General Gates made an excellent disposition of his forces to stop the enemy's way. He selected ground which was so situated that the elevation of a part of it, together with deep ravines in other parts, and a series of intrenchments which he threw up where the ground was level, formed a long line of formidable obstructions, extending to some distance back from the river. Here General Burgoyne advanced to attack him on the 19th of September. An obstinate battle was fought, the result of which was, that the Americans held their ground, and though they lost many men, the British lost many more, and failed entirely in their attempt to force their passage.

Burgoyne fell back after the battle to a stronger position, where he intrenched himself, and the two armies remained inactive for many days.

BATTLE OF STILLWATER

Burgoyne made every possible effort to send word down to New York, to General Clinton, who was in command there, to inform him of his desperate situation, and to urge him to send up a force to relieve him; but the American pickets and sentinels kept up so close a watch upon all the avenues of egress as to render all communication impossible.

In the meantime the British army were gradually coming to the end of their scanty store of provisions, while the numbers, and the strength, and confidence of the Americans were increasing every day.

At length, after many operations and maneuvers which cannot be here fully detailed, another great battle was fought, which is generally known as the battle of Stillwater. It continued for two days, the 7th and 8th of October, and the result was, that Burgoyne's army was again defeated and driven back within their lines, with a loss of many hundred men. The Americans captured, too, many of the British guns, a number of tents, and a considerable quantity of ammunition.

DEATH AND BURIAL OF GENERAL FRASER

One of the most serious of the losses which the British army sustained on this occasion, was in the death of General Fraser, one of Burgoyne's most valuable officers. He was mortally wounded by the American sharpshooters while he was on duty in the field with some officers of his staff. Just before he was struck himself, a ball cut the crupper of his saddle, and another, passing just before him, went through his horse's mane. Those around him warned him that probably the enemy were taking special aim at him, and urged him to move away—but he deemed it important that he should remain at his post, and a moment afterward he fell mortally wounded, and was carried into the camp.

He died that night; but before he died, he requested to be buried on a mound within a certain redoubt which formed a part of the works which the Americans were assailing. His body remained covered with a sheet, in the tent where he died, during all the next day, while the battle was still going on. At length, at six o'clock preparations were made for the burial, according to the request of the dying man; and a small party, headed by the chaplain, proceeded in funeral procession to the mound.

The Americans observed them, and not knowing in what duty they were engaged, opened fire upon them; and during a portion of the time while the chaplain was reading the burial service, cannon balls were striking here and there all around the spot. The earth thrown up by one of the balls fell upon the chaplain, Mr. Brudenell, and also upon the body—as if the demon of carnage wished to take part in its own terrible way, in the holy ceremony enjoined by the rubric of the episcopal church, of laying "dust to dust, and ashes to ashes."

At length, however, the Americans discovered what the state of the case was, and they immediately ceased the cannonading, but began soon to fire, at solemn intervals, a minute-gun, in token of respectful recognition of the ceremony, and in honor of the deceased. These guns were continued until the service was concluded and the party had retired.

LADY HARRIET ACKLAND

Perhaps the most romantic of the incidents which occurred during this memorable campaign are those connected with the story of Lady Harriet Ackland, the wife of Major Sir Francis Ackland, one of Burgoyne's most prominent officers. She was a lady of the highest rank and station, and had been accustomed in England to all the refinements and elegances of the very best English society. She, however, accompanied her husband to America, and kept herself as near to him all the time during the progress of the campaign as could be allowed; so that when he was sick, or in trouble of any kind, she could always come to him with very little delay. Of course, in doing this, she was subjected to privations, hardships, and exposures of the severest kind.

She was in the British camp during the battles of the 7th and 8th of October just described, and in the midst of all the confusion and dismay produced in the British army in their falling back from the battleground, she learned that her husband was wounded and a prisoner in the hands of the Americans.

THE CAPTURE OF MAJOR ACKLAND

Major Ackland was shot through the legs on the afternoon of the first day of the fight, and had succeeded in crawling for shelter into one of the angles of a zigzag fence near, when some American officers passing by, found him lying there, and an American boy near him just taking aim at him to shoot him. They ordered the boy off and caused Major Ackland to be conveyed to the American camp, where of course he was held as a prisoner, though he received all the attention which his rank, and his condition as a wounded man, demanded.

As soon as Lady Ackland learned this she sent a request to General Burgoyne to allow her to make the attempt to pass into the American lines to find her husband. General Burgoyne was in the midst of a scene of the greatest excitement and confusion when she made this request, but he was so much touched by the heroic devotedness to her husband which such a resolution implied—

especially considering that Lady Ackland had been all day exposed to a drenching rain, and was almost exhausted with want of food, and of rest, that he at once seized a scrap of paper which lay at hand and wrote upon it as follows.

General Burgoyne's Letter to General Gates

"Sir,—Lady Harriet Ackland, a lady of the first distinction of family, rank and personal virtues, is under such concern on account of Major Ackland her husband, wounded, and a prisoner in your hands that I cannot refuse her request to commit her to your protection. Whatever general impropriety there may be, in persons in my situation and yours to solicit favors, I cannot see the uncommon perseverance in every female grace and exaltation of character of this lady, and her very hard fortune, without testifying that your attentions to her will lay me under obligations.

"I am sir, your obedient servant,
"J. Burgoyne."

We readily see in the confused and somewhat incoherent style of this communication marks of the agitation and embarrassment of mind, and the circumstances of hurry and confusion under which it was written.

Down the River in a Boat

Although Lady Ackland was faint with hunger, thirst and fatigue, General Burgoyne had nothing whatever to offer her for refreshment. Someone procured her a little rum diluted with turbid water brought from the nearest pool. General Burgoyne ordered a boat to be immediately made ready, and furnished with men to row, and in this boat she set out just after sunset to go down the river to the American lines in the midst of a driving storm of wind and rain.

She had with her her own maid and her husband's servant, though the last was entirely helpless, having gone to the battlefield during the day to search for his master among the dead and wounded while the firing was still going on; and having himself been wounded by one of the balls. Besides these, the chaplain, Mr. Brudenel, who volunteered to accompany her, was also in the boat.

The boat pushed off, and the party went on down the river through the increasing darkness and storm for some miles, until they had passed entirely beyond the scene of the conflict between the two armies, and had reached the ground which was in the undisputed possession of the Americans. Here they turned in toward the shore. The danger now was that the pickets stationed on the bank would fire upon them without warning, as they would have perhaps been justified in doing on hearing a boat passing down the river in the dark. But they did not do so. The sentinel who first heard the sound of the oars hailed them. Lady Ackland answered the summons herself—thinking that if they heard a woman's voice, they would be less likely to fire.

The sentinel was alarmed on hearing her reply. He could see nothing, and to hear a female voice coming from out over the stormy water, in so dark and tempestuous a night, called up at once to his mind the idea of a ghost, or some other supernatural object of terror. He, however, after first calling one of his comrades, allowed the boat to come to the land. On hearing Lady Ackland's story, he found it so incredible that he believed the party were spies, and so he detained them where they were until he could send to his commanding officer, Major Dearborn, for instructions.

Major Dearborn, as soon as he understood the case, immediately did everything in his power to relieve Lady Ackland's distress, and to accomplish her wishes. He invited her to his quarters, gave her tea and other refreshments, and then sent her under a suitable escort to the part of the camp where her husband was, and thus she rejoined him.

BARONESS RIEDESEL

Among the other European ladies who accompanied their husbands on this expedition, was the Baroness Riedesel, the wife of General Riedesel, who commanded one of the corps of German troops that the English subsidized for this war. These ladies all supposed, it seems, as their husbands also did, that there would be very little opposition made to Burgoyne's advance. The royalists were so numerous, they thought, in the country which they were to pass through, and the terror of the other inhabitants would be so much excited by the Indian auxiliaries that accompanied the expedition, that there would be but little resistance attempted. The campaign pictured itself to their imaginations in the light of a triumphal progress which would only present to them a series of romantic but agreeable adventures, exciting to witness, and charming to recount to their friends on their return.

With this general feeling, however, there was doubtless mingled in the mind of each of the ladies some apprehension of possible difficulty and danger for her husband, in which the loving attention of a devoted wife might be of great value.

Hardships and Sufferings of the Baroness

During the last few days before Burgoyne surrendered, when his retreat was cut off, and every part of the ground which his forces occupied was under fire, the exposures and sufferings of these ladies were terrible. Their husbands could do nothing for them, being either wholly absorbed in their dreadful work upon the field, or else perhaps wounded or made prisoners. When the last series of conflicts came on, the baroness was in a certain house in the town of Saratoga, which is still preserved and is known as the Riedesel house. Before long the approach of the Americans and the progress of the battle brought this house under fire, which fire was the more severe, as the Americans, seeing many persons coming and going about the place, supposed it was the headquarters of the officers, whereas there was none within it but wounded men, and women and children. The baroness had with her three young children of her own.

The shots striking in and around the house soon drove all the inmates to seek refuge in the cellar. They remained here in great terror and distress all day, from time to time hearing the cannon balls crash through the house above them, and roll away over the ground beyond. The baroness crouched down in one corner, while her children lay by her side upon the cold ground, with their heads in her lap, and slept.

There were three other ladies in the cellar, and also several officers who were dreadfully wounded. They tried to partition off small spaces in the corners by putting up curtains, in order to afford the ladies some semblance of seclusion. They were in momentary fear of the house being set on fire by hot shot or shells, or of an irruption of the enemy upon them. They suffered very much for want of water; for if anyone attempted to go down to the river to procure a supply, he was immediately made the target of a multitude of guns. At last, however, a soldier's wife was found, who was willing to go to the river, on the presumption that the Americans would not fire upon a woman.

Her opinion of the humanity of the American soldiers proved correct. They allowed her to go and come for water without molesting her.

The baroness and those who were with her remained in this dreadful situation for *six days!* when at length they were released by the cessation of hostilities which preceded the surrender. The baroness was soon afterward conveyed to the American camp, where she and her children were received by General Schuyler, and treated with the greatest kindness.

THE BARONESS RIEDESEL'S JOURNEY

The baroness wrote a very minute and extremely graphic account of these scenes, and of the trials and sufferings which she experienced in passing through them. Her narration closes in the following words:

"Some days after this we arrived in Albany, where we had so often wished ourselves; but we did not enter it—as we expected we should—victors. We were received by the good General Schuyler, his wife and daughters—not as enemies, but as kind friends. They treated us with the most marked attention, as they did General Burgoyne, who had caused General Schuyler's beautifully-finished house to be burned. In fact they behaved like persons of exalted minds, who determined to bury all recollections of their own injuries in a contemplation of our misfortunes. General Burgoyne was struck with General Schuyler's generosity, and said to him, "You show me great kindness, although I have done you much injury."

"That was the fate of war," replied the brave man, "let us say no more about it."

But to return to the story.

Burgoyne's Last Council of War

General Burgoyne continued to struggle despairingly against the terrible difficulties of his situation for nearly a week after all reasonable ground of hope had disappeared. He was entirely surrounded; every avenue of escape was cut off, and the circle of fire which environed him had been drawing in upon him more and more closely, until his whole camp was now commanded by the guns of the enemy, and there was no place where even the wounded could be sheltered, or even a council could be held in safety. At last he was compelled to come to the conclusion that he must yield to his fate, and on the 13th of October he called a council of all his officers, to obtain their sanction for the surrender.

The deliberations of the council were very brief and hurried. Balls were flying about them all the time. The tent in which they were assembled was repeatedly perforated, and once an eighteen pound ball swept across the very table at which the generals were sitting. The conclusion was unanimous in favor of a surrender.

The Surrender

Accordingly a flag of truce was sent at once to General Gates, asking him to appoint a time to receive proposals, and he appointed ten o'clock the next morning. After various negotiations, a convention was agreed upon and signed.

The surrender was not an unconditional one—that is, the army of Burgoyne was not given up into the hands of the Americans to be held as prisoners of war, but the stipulations provided for their being marched across the country—of course, after being disarmed— to Boston, there to be embarked on vessels which the British government should provide for the purpose, and sent home to the several countries where the different classes of troops belonged—on the express condition, however, that they were not to serve again against the Americans during the war.

The officers were to be released on their parole, and allowed to proceed down the river to Albany and thence to New York.

The arms, ammunition and stores, of course, were to be delivered to the Americans as their lawful prize. There were nearly fifty pieces of cannon, five thousand muskets, seventy thousand cartridges and other things in proportion.

The number of men that were surrendered were nearly six thousand. There were, however, more than twice that number of Americans surrounding them when the surrender was made.

MARCH OF THE CAPTURED TROOPS TO BOSTON

The march of this vast body of disarmed and helpless men to Boston formed one of the most extraordinary and imposing spectacles of the war. They were escorted by a small body of American troops. They marched, however, under the immediate direction of their own officers, their usual military organization being maintained. The people of the country flocked to see them as they passed, but no insult or indignity of any kind was offered to them. On the contrary they were everywhere treated with commiseration and kindness.

Some serious difficulties and delays arose, before these troops were finally embarked for Europe, arising from misunderstandings which cannot be here fully explained. In due time, however, they all, together with General Burgoyne, General Riedesel, Major Ackland and the other principal officers found their way to England.

SEQUEL OF THE STORY OF LADY ACKLAND

Major Ackland and his family were accompanied by Mr. Brudenel, the chaplain who had evinced so much courage and such devotedness to Lady Ackland in the time of her extreme danger and distress. Some time after the return of the party to England Major Ackland lost his life in a duel, and his wife was so much overwhelmed with this affliction that she lost her reason, and was for two years insane. At length, partly through the watchful care and kind attentions of the chaplain the balance of her mind was restored, and in the end, a strong mutual attachment sprang up between them and they were married.

EFFECT OF THE SURRENDER OF BURGOYNE

The great victory of Gates over Burgoyne, involving as it did the capture of his entire army by the Americans, and the complete recovery of the whole region which had been the scene of the campaign, produced a very great sensation throughout the country and exerted a vast influence, both in Europe and America, in determining the final result of the war. The effect in Europe was even greater than in America. It greatly strengthened the hands of that portion of the English Parliament and English people that had opposed the war, and embarrassed the ministers in respect to future measures for carrying it on.

RECOGNITION OF AMERICAN INDEPENDENCE
BY FRANCE

The most important of the results of the victory was, however, its influence upon the policy of France. The French government had secretly favored the American cause from the beginning, and had even offered some furtive aid; but they did not dare to take open ground in favor of the insurgents till they could see how they were likely to succeed. Congress had sent commissioners to France some time before this, and they had been endeavoring to negotiate a treaty with the French government to acknowledge the independence of the Americans, and aid them in the war. The French king, however, and his ministers, delayed taking any decided and open action, preferring to wait for a time, and watch the course of events. The news of the surrender of Burgoyne at once decided them. They openly received the commissioners, framed and ratified a treaty of alliance, in which the government of France publicly acknowledged the independence of America, and pledged itself to render vigorous aid in compelling England to acknowledge it, and not to lay down their arms until the effect was secured.

This treaty was concluded in February, 1778, and preparations were at once made to send out a large fleet and a considerable body of troops to cooperate with the Americans in carrying on the war.

The people now began universally to believe that their independence was sure.

CHAPTER VIII
OCCUPATION OF PHILADELPHIA

A Serious Reverse

In the meantime, while in the north, the American cause had made so important an advance by the great victory gained by the armies under Schuyler and Gates over the grand expedition of Burgoyne, farther south the fortune of war had been, and for a long time continued to be, extremely unfavorable. The first of the disasters which befell the American arms in this direction was the loss of Philadelphia, together with that of all the country around, which was successfully invaded by a British expedition which arrived there from New York about the time that Burgoyne's difficulties and embarrassments on the banks of the Hudson were commencing.

Expedition Sent to Philadelphia

The expedition which attacked Philadelphia consisted of a fleet of ships conveying a land force of eighteen thousand men. It sailed from New York in the middle of the summer of 1777, the year of Burgoyne's campaign. The fleet was under the command of Admiral Howe, and the land force under that of his brother, General Sir William Howe—the officers who had been so successful in their operations against New York, as related in a former chapter.

Landing of the Expedition

It had been the intention of General Howe to take his force up the Delaware River, so as to approach Philadelphia with the fleet directly from the sea—but he learned on his arrival in Delaware Bay that the passage up the river, besides being guarded by strong fortifications on the banks, was barred by formidable obstructions in the channel which it would be very difficult for the fleet to break through. So he concluded to go on and ascend Chesapeake Bay instead, from the head of which he could march by land across the intervening territory and so approach Philadelphia from the southern side. This movement was successfully accomplished, and the whole force was landed in safety, on the 25th of August, near the mouth of the river Elk, at the head of Chesapeake Bay, fifty or sixty miles southwest of Philadelphia.

THE PROCLAMATION

There was no force there to oppose the landing, but General Howe was delayed some days by stormy weather, and by the necessity of procuring another means of transportation for his provisions and baggage across the land. During this interval he issued a proclamation to the inhabitants, inviting them to return to their duty as subjects of the king, and promising protection to all who should come in and surrender themselves, and take the oath of allegiance.

The proclamation had no effect. The people with one accord combined to resist the invaders. They organized themselves into militia companies, and prepared to do everything in their power to embarrass General Howe's operations, and impede his march, although they were aware that they could do nothing effectual to oppose him, until the regular army under Washington arrived.

ADVANCE OF WASHINGTON

We left Washington in the spring of this year in New Jersey, where he had been successfully engaged in expelling the British from that state. As soon as he heard of Howe's landing, he crossed the Delaware and advanced to meet him. The two armies came together on the banks of the river Brandywine which, as may been by the map,[1] is a small stream flowing into the Delaware River a little south of Philadelphia.

---

[1]See map on p. 78.

THE BATTLE OF BRANDYWINE

Here on the 11th of September 1777, a protracted and obstinate battle was fought, the result of which was decidedly against the Americans. Indeed it could hardly have been expected to be otherwise, for the Americans brought into the field only about eleven thousand men, and of these many were fresh recruits just enlisted, and the others were more or less exhausted by their long and hurried march from New Jersey. The British force on the other hand was eighteen thousand strong.

Washington, however, felt bound, notwithstanding these disadvantages, to make an attempt to arrest the progress of the enemy, knowing very well that if he were to abandon the defense of Philadelphia without a struggle, the country would be greatly disappointed and much discouraged.

The American army fell back in considerable disorder from the banks of the Brandywine after the battle, leaving the way to Philadelphia open to the conquerors. General Howe immediately marched on and took possession of the city. In the meantime, however, Congress, anticipating this result, had removed the hospitals, magazines, public stores, and all other national property, to places of security in the interior, and had adjourned to Lancaster, a town situated about seventy or eighty miles to the westward of Philadelphia.

General Howe did not lead his whole force into the city, but taking two or three regiments there, he marched the rest to Germantown, which, as will be seen by the map, lies a few miles to the northward, and established a permanent camp for them there.

THE BATTLE OF GERMANTOWN

As soon as General Washington had recovered from the effects of his defeat on the Brandywine, and had obtained the necessary reinforcements, he formed a plan for attacking the British camp in Germantown. But the plan was not destined to succeed. The American army advanced in four columns, marching all night with the intention of surprising the camp before it was light in the morning. The surprise itself was successful, but after a protracted and obstinate struggle the Americans were beaten off and were obliged to retreat in confusion, with a loss of a thousand men.

THE DELAWARE FORTS

The victory of the British and their possession of the ground was now complete, except that the Americans still held possession of the forts on the Delaware, just below the city, which commanded the channel at the points where the obstructions had been laid. The British ships were thus prevented from coming up the river, and were cut off from the only channel of communication by which supplies could be brought up to the army during the coming winter. It was very necessary for them therefore to reduce these forts and remove the obstructions in order to make their position in Philadelphia tenable.

The principal forts were Fort Mifflin and Fort Mercer, which, as will be seen by the map, were situated at the confluence of the Delaware and Schuylkill some miles below Philadelphia. Preparations were accordingly made as soon as possible for an attack on these forts with an overwhelming force, one from the river and the other from the land. The Americans determined to defend them to the last extremity.

THE FIRST ATTACKS REPULSED

Fort Mercer, on the New Jersey shore, was attacked by a large body of Hessians under the command of Count Donop, on the land side. They first sent a herald with a drummer and a flag of truce, up to the walls, to demand the surrender of the fort. The herald called out,

> "The king of England orders his rebellious subjects to lay down their arms, and if they stand the battle no quarters whatever will be given."

Colonel Greene, the American officer in command, replied that they did not ask for quarters and would not give any.

The Hessians then came on and made a terrific onslaught upon the fort, and so close was the conflict for some time that some of the dead bodies of the Hessians that were left upon the ground, were found with the flesh penetrated by the wadding of the guns. The result was, however, that the Americans were triumphantly victorious. The Hessians were driven back headlong. Their commander, Count Donop, and many hundreds of the men were killed, and the rest fled in confusion.

It was substantially the same with Fort Mifflin, though this last was built upon an island, and was accordingly attacked by ships of war from the river. The ships had passed down the Chesapeake and up the Delaware for this purpose. There were two frigates and some other vessels. The attack, however, totally failed. The fire from the fort was so heavy that the ships could not endure it. One of the frigates was struck with a red hot shot from the fort, and was set on fire. In the confusion, which this occasioned, the ship drifted upon a sandbank, where at length the fire reached the magazine and the ship was blown up, producing a tremendous explosion.

Not long afterward the other frigate was struck and destroyed in the same manner, and then the rest of the vessels withdrew down the river, leaving the Americans for a time in undisputed possession of the forts.

FINAL REDUCTION OF THE FORTS

The Americans, however, did not long enjoy the fruits of their victory. It was almost absolutely essential to the British army in Philadelphia that the passage up the river from the sea for their ships should be opened, and General Howe, finding that the assaults failed, immediately commenced a system of measures more deliberate but more sure. He advanced cautiously and erected formidable batteries for cannonading the forts. He cut new channels among the islands below, and brought up through them a great number of ships of war, and gun boats armed and equipped especially for the service. At length, on the 10th of November, two or three weeks after the first assaults had been made, his preparations were complete and he opened fire. The bombardment was continued for ten days. The garrisons made desperate efforts to maintain their ground, but their efforts were unavailing. For a time they repaired at night, as well as they could, the damage done by day, but they soon became exhausted with these efforts. The ramparts were breached and battered on every side, guns were dismounted, magazines were blown up, and at length both forts, first Fort Mifflin and then Fort Mercer, were compelled to surrender. Most of the men made their escape, and a number of American vessels that were lying above the forts succeeded in stealing past Philadelphia on a dark night and so avoiding capture. Others that could not thus be saved were set on fire and abandoned.

The British immediately dismantled and destroyed the forts, removed the obstructions from the river, and then their ships at once came up to town.

WITHDRAWAL OF THE AMERICAN ARMY

General Washington, after having been thus compelled to yield the ground to the enemy, spent some weeks in reassembling and reorganizing his forces, repairing damages, making arrangements for procuring supplies, and also in considering the feasibility of an attack upon the British in Philadelphia, or of some other hostile operations against them during the time that remained of the season. He finally concluded that there was nothing more that could be done, and that it only remained for him to make arrangements for going into winter quarters in some convenient spot where he might keep his army together until spring.

For this purpose he wished to find some place that would at once afford shelter from the cold and the storms of the winter, and at the same time one that could be easily made defensible against the enemy. It was necessary also that it should be in some convenient position not very far from the city, where he could watch the operations of the enemy, prevent his obtaining supplies from the country around, and protect the inhabitants from any hostile excursions that he might undertake.

He chose finally a place called Valley Forge, which, as will be seen by the map, is on the west side of the Schuylkill, twenty-five or thirty miles from Philadelphia.

Destitute Condition of the Troops

The condition of the American army on its arrival at Valley Forge, which was about the middle of December, when the winter was already beginning to set in, was pitiable in the extreme. The soldiers were almost entirely destitute of clothes, shoes, food, fuel, and of almost everything else necessary not merely for comfort, but for existence. One of the most trying of their wants was that of covering for their feet. Their shoes were worn out, and there were no means of procuring fresh supplies. Multitudes of men were barefooted, and the last twenty miles of their march to Valley Forge was marked by a long bloody track through the snow. Washington made exertions to procure some sort of protection to the feet of his men by moccasins made of raw hides, but notwithstanding all that could be done the destitution and suffering were extreme.

The Darkest Period of the Revolution

In fact this season and the winter which followed it, that is the winter of 1777–1778, was in some respect the darkest period in the history of the revolution, or rather it was the period of the greatest difficulty and distress though not that of the greatest discouragement or danger. The capture of Burgoyne's army had indeed greatly encouraged and inspirited the country, and it had laid the foundation, as has already been stated, for a treaty with the French government, which resulted in the following spring in the sending out from France of an expedition which gave to the cause of independence very able and efficient support. But none of these substantial advantages of Gates's victory had yet been realized, and in the meantime the resources of Congress were exhausted; the troops had consumed all their stores and supplies; the country was distracted by conflicts between the partisans of the different leading generals, and the cause seemed to be on the brink of ruin.

The Encampment at Valley Forge

Washington bore up against the difficulties of his situation with a firmness and perseverance truly heroic. As soon as the army reached the camping ground at Valley Forge he commenced the building of a regular system of log huts to furnish shelter during the winter both for officers and men.

The men were divided into parties of twelve, each party being supplied with proper tools, and all those whose remaining clothes were sufficient to allow of their exposing themselves in the open wintry air were sent into the forests around to procure the necessary materials and drag them to the camp. The camp itself was laid out regularly like the streets of a city, with a place allotted to each hut. The huts were fourteen feet by sixteen in dimension. The sides were built of logs, the roofs of rude slabs or planks formed by splitting straight grained logs by means of axes and wedges. There was a fireplace in each but it was built of wood, no other material being at hand. The sides of the fireplace were guarded from the effects of the heat by being plastered over thickly with clay, a protection which would have been wholly insufficient for any but the very low and smoldering fires which were all that the resources of the camp could afford.

There was wood in the forests, it is true, but there were few tools to cut it, and no beasts of burden to bring it in. During the winter the men were often compelled to yoke themselves together and draw, on rude sleds which they made themselves, the necessary supplies for the camp, or to load them as burdens upon their backs. To perform such services moreover, they were obliged to borrow each other's shoes and clothes.

There was great difficulty too in procuring supplies even for these miserable modes of transportation. A great number of the farmers in the neighborhood were British "sympathizers," and would not sell their produce at any rate. Others refused to take the congressional paper money—the greenbacks of those days—which constituted the only circulating medium. In consequence of these and other causes the soldiers were reduced in the course of the winter to a condition of scarcity little short of absolute famine.

The army continued to occupy this encampment, with very little alleviation of their condition, during the whole of the winter of 1777–8. Washington felt for them very acutely, and often expressed wonder at the patience and fortitude with which they bore their privations and sufferings. He himself was incessantly occupied in efforts to obtain supplies, and to relieve the wants of his men. For a time, until they were somewhat comfortably sheltered in their huts, he lived among them in a tent, but when the huts were finished he made his headquarters in a small farmhouse nearby.

The whole number of men that were thus encamped at Valley Forge was about twelve thousand, of whom, however, nearly one quarter were at the beginning unfit for duty from the effects of exhaustion, sickness, or want, and this number became largely increased as the winter went on. Before the spring came, however, their hearts were cheered by the news which arrived of the treaty which had been made with France, and new and buoyant hopes arose in their minds of better times soon to come.

ALARM OF THE ENGLISH GOVERNMENT

For, in the meantime, while the American armies were enduring these sufferings, the negotiations with France referred to in the last chapter were going on, and at length, by midwinter, a treaty was signed, and preparations at once began to be made for sending out a fleet from France, in the spring, to render the Americans the necessary aid. These proceedings alarmed the English government exceedingly. They immediately began to make vigorous efforts for conciliating the colonies, as they still termed them, and effecting a peace before the French should have time to interfere. They passed various bills, the purport of which was to grant to the Americans all that they had asked for at the beginning of the war, and they appointed a board of commissioners to come to America and endeavor to persuade the people to lay down their arms and give up the plan of independence, on condition of having all their other demands substantially complied with.

TOO LATE

But after hearing these proposals and calmly considering them, the Americans replied that it was too late. They could not now listen to any proposals for peace, that were not based on an acknowledgment of their independence.

EVACUATION OF PHILADELPHIA

As the spring drew near, the British general, Sir Henry Clinton, who in the course of the winter had taken the place of General Howe as the officer in command at Philadelphia, began to fear that the French fleet which was expected to arrive on the coast before long, might enter the Delaware, and so shut him in and cut off his supplies; and that then Washington might increase his forces on the land side so as to surround him entirely and perhaps capture his whole army. He accordingly determined to evacuate Philadelphia and march back through New Jersey to New York. He kept his plans so profoundly secret, however, that Washington had no knowledge of his intentions, until one day about the middle of June he heard that the British general had actually crossed the Delaware with all his army and commenced his march to the northward. Washington immediately set out with his whole force in pursuit of him.

THE BATTLE OF MONMOUTH

Washington crossed the Delaware at or near Trenton, the British army being to the eastward between him and the sea. Washington's forces had been largely augmented during the spring, and bodies of militia too were rising in various parts of the country, and hastening to join him, so that the British were considerably outnumbered, and were in great danger of being surrounded and cut off. They, however, pushed on as rapidly as possible, the Americans following them closely, hovering upon their left flank, harassing their march, and crowding them toward the sea. At length the two armies reached Monmouth,[1] where the British were brought to bay, and an obstinate and bloody battle was fought—one of the most celebrated of the battles of the war.

The day on which the battle of Monmouth was fought was Sunday the 28th of June. The sky was cloudless, the air was calm, and the sun was so hot that nearly sixty of the British soldiers died during the day from the heat and the fatigue which they endured, without being wounded at all. Many of the Americans perished in the same way.

---

[1]See map on p. 78.

The battle was not decisive though the British troops suffered the heaviest losses. When night came the Americans lay down upon their arms, in the field, to sleep, intending to renew and finish their work on the following day. But when morning came they found that the British army had disappeared. They had stolen away secretly and silently in the night, and before they could be overtaken they made their way to Sandy Hook, where they found a fleet of transports ready to receive them, and convey them to New York.

Re-Possession of Philadelphia

Of course the evacuation of Philadelphia by the British troops left the city open again to the Americans, and General Washington sent a small body of troops to take possession of it. He also appointed General Arnold military governor of the city and placed him in command.

General Arnold had been wounded in the battles fought with Burgoyne just before his surrender, and on that account was not able to go into active service in the field; and although he was known to be a very unprincipled man, still he had acted in so brave and energetic a manner, and had rendered such essential service to the American cause on many occasions, that General Washington thought it right to nominate him to this post.

Arnold a Bad Boy

Although General Arnold had an excellent mother, he seems in early life to have been a bad boy, and he exhibited when quite young those traits of desperate and daring recklessness, which afterward made him so renowned. At one time he and the other boys got possession of an old cannon which had been spiked and could not be fired in the usual way, so they set it up on end in the ground, like a post, and then after loading it Arnold fired it by dropping a burning coal into the muzzle. At another time when he and the other boys had stolen some barrels to make a bonfire, and a constable or a policeman came after them to take the barrels away, Arnold fell into a great rage, threw off his jacket, doubled up his fists, and dared the constable to fight him.

When he was a young man his sister was engaged to be married to a Frenchman whom he disliked, and Arnold ordered him not to come to the house. The Frenchman paid no attention to this warning and so when he did come Arnold shot at him with a pistol, and the Frenchman barely escaped with his life by leaping out of the window.

ARNOLD A GOOD SOLDIER

Unfortunately a bad man often makes a very good soldier, and Arnold, though he seems to have become more and more reckless and unprincipled as he grew up, yet, when he finally joined the American army, became a very efficient and energetic officer, and was always ready to engage in the most daring and desperate undertakings. It is true he was very insubordinate and unmanageable, and was continually getting himself into difficulty with those around him, whether above or beneath him in rank. Still, with all his faults, he had on many occasions shown so much bravery, and had evinced such ardor and zeal in the American cause, that Washington thought it best to give him the post of governor of Philadelphia, since, while performing the duties of that office, he could remain in a state of comparative repose until his wound should be healed.

Arnold's residence, in Philadelphia, in fulfillment of this appointment, became subsequently quite memorable in American history from the fact that his defection from the cause of his countrymen, and his going over to the British under circumstances which made him so renowned as the great American traitor, probably originated in events that occurred then and there.

HIS MARRIAGE

One of these events was his marriage with a lady who was the daughter of a Philadelphia merchant, and who, with all her family, had given her sympathies entirely to the British side in this quarrel. The name of the lady was Margaret Shippen. She was Arnold's second wife, and was much younger than her husband. He seemed to become devotedly attached to her, but the marriage excited much surprise and some displeasure among Arnold's American friends, for not only was her father a strong partisan of the English, but she herself personally had evinced a very decided sympathy for the royalist cause. She had taken a very active part in the festivities with which the Tory families of Philadelphia had welcomed General Howe when he entered Philadelphia in the preceding autumn, and also in the farewell parties given to the British officers when the army went away in the spring.

The other American officers, who had not yet had time to forget the dreadful exposures and sufferings they had endured during their winter in Valley Forge, were not a little indignant that their commander should choose for his wife a fashionable belle, who, while they were enduring such terrible extremes of want and privation in their encampment, was lavishing her blandishments upon their enemies, and the enemies of their country, in the city from which they had been expelled.

Arnold's Pecuniary Difficulties

Anther circumstance, which, it was supposed, conspired with the influence of his wife to lead Arnold to the commission of the great crime of which he was afterward guilty, was the extravagant style of living which he adopted in Philadelphia, and the consequent hopeless pecuniary embarrassment in which he became involved. It is a long story, which cannot be here related in full, but the substance of it is that he took a large and splendid mansion, kept servants in livery and a coach in four, and gave splendid parties and entertainments of all kinds.

To raise money for these purposes he resorted to various malpractices in his government, which led to charges being made against him on which he was tried and condemned by a court-martial. His sentence was to be reprimanded. Washington administered the reprimand in the most gentle and considerate manner, but the result of the whole affair was to exasperate Arnold and prepare him for the course which he subsequently pursued. His defection, however, did not actually take place till about two years after this time.

HIS FINAL PLAN

The reason for this delay seems to have been that Arnold could not succeed any sooner in placing himself in a situation to make his treason sufficiently advantageous to the British to enable them to pay the high price which he demanded for it. Of course the value of the reward which he could expect for going over to the enemy would depend upon the nature and extent of the advantages which he could secure to them by his defection, and the plan which, after mature deliberation, Arnold resolved upon was to procure for himself the appointment of commander of the post of West Point,[1] which was then simply a strong fortress among the highlands on the Hudson River about fifty miles from New York. The British had possession of the lower part of the river and had their ships of war at anchor there, while the Americans held the country above. The fortress at West Point, and some others among the Highlands near it and dependent upon it, formed the chief obstacle to the advance of the British in that direction, and Arnold thought that if he could obtain the command of that fortress he might make excellent terms with the British for delivering it into their hands, since that would give them the command of the river, and open the way for them to penetrate far into the interior of the state.

During all the while that he had been forming these plans he had been in secret correspondence with Sir Henry Clinton, who was the commander-in-chief of the British forces at this time, and had undoubtedly acted with his concurrence in everything which he had done. The communications were carried on through Major Andre, a young English officer who had formed a particular friendship with his wife in Philadelphia, before her marriage, and had continued the friendship subsequently by correspondence.

At length after much maneuvering and many earnest solicitations, accompanied with the most zealous professions of devotedness to the American cause, Arnold succeeded in the summer of 1780 in obtaining his appointment as commander of the fortress of West Point, and of all its dependencies on the banks of the river below; and he immediately commenced his negotiations and arrangements <u>for surrendering</u> the whole into the hands of the British general.

[1] See map on p. 18.

The Negotiation

It was necessary to manage the correspondence and the negotiations with the utmost caution and secrecy. In bargainings for treason and fraud, of course, neither party can place the least reliance upon the honor of the other, and Clinton could not know but that Arnold was arranging some deep-laid stratagem to entrap *him*. At length, however, after a great deal of management and maneuvering and many mysterious letters under feigned names sent to and fro, a personal interview was appointed between Andre and Arnold at a retired place on the bank of the river just below the American lines, in order finally to agree upon the terms and close the bargain. Arnold came down the river by land, and Andre was brought up from one of the English men-of-war in a boat which Arnold sent down for him under a flag of truce, which pretended to have some other errand.

The Meeting

The meeting took place at night in a very solitary place near a small creek or cove which here opened from the river. The boat which had brought Andre to the place remained in the cove ready to take him back again. The man who had accompanied Arnold waited too, in a thicket near, with two horses—one for himself and one for the general, ready to take him up the river again to his quarters among the forts, after the conference was ended.

Andre Becomes a Spy

Thus far Andre had incurred no special risk excepting that of being captured and so made a prisoner of war, for he was yet without the American lines. He wore his uniform, but it was covered with a cloak. But for some reason or other the conference was protracted so long that the morning came before it was concluded. There were in fact still a great many details to be arranged. Finally, after much doubt and hesitation, Andre allowed himself to be persuaded to mount one of the horses and proceed with Arnold up the river a few miles to a certain house, where they could complete the business with

Conference between Arnold and Andre.

more security. In doing this Andre had to pass the post sentinels that marked the American lines, and by that act became a spy, subject, if taken, to be hanged instead of being treated as a prisoner of war.

Conclusion of the Story

The sad termination of this story—sad so far as poor Andre was concerned, but joyous and triumphant for the American cause— is well known. In the course of the day the negotiations were all completed, and the necessary papers put into Andre's hands, and by him ingeniously concealed in his boots. He set out on his return, but found when he came to the place where he was to embark in the boat, that the British ship had been fired upon by some batteries on the shore, and forced to go down the river. The boatmen refused to follow her down. Andre was then compelled to undertake to make his way down to New York by land, and he crossed the river in order to go down on the eastern side. He went on very safely until he reached the very last of the American outposts, but there he was stopped by the picket guard, searched and arrested. By the papers which were found upon his person the whole plot was discovered, but before General Washington had time to take measures for the arrest of Arnold he made his escape. The forts however and strongholds which he had intended to betray, were saved.

Execution of Major Andre

Very great efforts were made by the British government to save Major Andre's life, and even the Americans almost universally pitied his hard fate, and wished that he might be spared. But the authorities decided, after full and careful consideration of the case, that the stern demands of military necessity required that he should die, and he was accordingly executed.

Arnold

As for Arnold, the British government in their reception and treatment of him, felt bound to reward the intended treachery, though they despised the man. They gave him a commission in their army, and paid him fifty thousand dollars in money. He fought several campaigns afterward against the Americans, but was an object of contempt and aversion wherever he went, and after drifting about the world for some years universally despised, he died at last in the West Indies. His memory is utterly execrated by the Americans, and is regarded as infamous by all mankind.

as convoy to the transports in which the soldiers were conveyed.

The expedition sailed from New York near the end of November, and the fleet was about four weeks in making the passage. Such a squadron of course proceeds very slowly on account of the hindrances and delays occasioned by the necessity of keeping together. The speed of the slowest and most sluggish of the vessels must necessarily regulate the progress of all the rest.

The ships arrived off the mouth of the Savannah River very near the end of December, where they were stopped by the vast series of shoals and sandbanks which gather around the outlet of the river, and form what is called the bar. Here they were detained nearly another week before the condition of the weather and the tide were such as to make it safe for them to attempt to go in.

PREPARATIONS OF THE AMERICANS

In the meantime the alarm had been given and the city of Savannah and the people of the surrounding country were thrown into a state of confusion and dismay. They were ill prepared to meet and repel such an enemy. The country was very thinly inhabited, and the population consisted moreover in great proportion of blacks who could not be trusted with arms. It was obviously not to be expected that a community like this could by any means produce, on a sudden call, such an uprising as that of the twenty thousand men who seized their arms and rushed to the environs of Boston on the alarm given by the battle of Lexington.

What was possible however was promptly done. There was a small force of about seven hundred men at Sunbury, thirty miles to the southward. These hastened at once to Savannah. Couriers were immediately despatched to Charleston in South Carolina to call for all the troops from that province that could be spared. Every effort was made too, though without much success, to procure men from the surrounding country.

EXCITEMENT IN SAVANNAH

In the city itself all was excitement and confusion. The archives of the government and all the public records were sent into the interior for safety. Many of the aged and infirm, and also of the women and children, were conveyed away, as well as such valuables belonging to private persons, as could be easily removed. The able-bodied men formed themselves into working parties, and commenced the construction of batteries, redoubts, and other means of defense below the city.

The American general, who was a North Carolinian, named Robert Howe, was earnest and indefatigable in his efforts to perfect the organization of his men, to increase their numbers by recruits from the interior, and to complete his arrangements and preparations. He could obtain, however, from the country only an addition of about two hundred to his numbers, so that when at length the British fleet succeeded in passing over the bar, and were coming up the river, he had a force of only about nine hundred men to oppose to them. The number of men under Colonel Campbell's command was over three thousand.

THE OPPOSING FORCES CONFRONT EACH OTHER

Perhaps if the Americans had known how vastly superior to theirs the force was which was advancing to attack them, they would have given up all hope of defending the city, and would have undertaken only to save their little army by a timely retreat. But Colonel Campbell had carefully concealed the amount of his force, and the American troops were accordingly brought down to make a stand against him. They were posted in line of battle below the city, the line being protected as much as possible by the intrenchments and other works which had been hastily constructed.

Colonel Campbell after some brief preliminary operations advanced with his main force toward this line. The Americans now for the first time perceived how formidable the force was with which they had to contend. They held a serious consultation on the question whether they should not retreat and abandon the town. They decided that it was too late to do this, and that nothing now remained for them but to take the chances of battle.

A Stratagem

Colonel Campbell had advanced with his forces directly toward the American lines, as if his intention had been to attack them openly in front, but he really entertained another design. He had learned in some way that there was an obscure pathway leading by a circuitous route among the swamps, and along the borders of the creeks and rice fields, by which a detachment might move secretly and gain the rear of the American army, so as not only to attack them in that quarter unexpectedly and simultaneously with the attack in front, and thus throw them into confusion, but also to cut off their retreat into the city in case of their defeat. He succeeded in procuring the services of a negro to guide the detachment along this path. The name of the negro was Quamino Dolly.

The Capture of Savannah

The plan thus formed was carried into execution and was entirely successful. The Americans soon discovered the double danger which threatened them and commenced a retreat. The only road by which they could reach Savannah traversed a swamp by means of a causeway. When they reached the causeway they found the enemy already there. A part succeeded in making their way over, before the preparations of the British to intercept them were complete. Others attempted to make their escape across the creeks and through the rice fields and swamps, and some who could swim succeeded, but of the rest great numbers were drowned, or were arrested in their progress by sinking in the mire, and were made prisoners. Those who succeeded in making their escape over the causeway were hotly pursued by the British into the town, and many of them were overtaken and bayoneted in the streets. The soldiers, in the mad excitement of their victory, for a time went on killing all whom they met, whether combatants or not, and several of the citizens who had taken no part in the hostilities were slain. Colonel Campbell however, as soon as he arrived, put an end to these outrages, and gave efficient protection to the persons and property of the inhabitants.

RETREAT OF THE AMERICAN ARMY

In the course of the conflict and of the flight nearly half of the American army were either killed or taken prisoners, or drowned in the creeks and morasses. The loss of the British was only about thirty.

The remnant of the Americans fled in extreme disorder into the interior, following the banks of the river Savannah, at the mouth of which the city stands. After going on for about eight miles, all in a state of hopeless confusion, they came to a ferry, where the men were rallied and some degree of order was restored, and then they crossed the river into South Carolina. The river here forms the boundary line.

THE STATE ENTIRELY SUBDUED

There were two other military posts of importance in the state, one at Sunbury and the other at Augusta. Expeditions were immediately sent out by the British general against these, and both were taken with very little resistance. The leading friends of independence throughout the state abandoned their homes and made their escape into South Carolina, and the mass of the inhabitants that remained having no means of continuing the struggle—a large proportion of them, in fact, having no inclination to do it—quietly submitted to their fate, and Georgia was considered as fully subdued.

Or rather the portion of the people that were the friends of the cause of independence were subdued, for the people were so nearly divided in opinion that the worst of their sufferings during the whole period of the war resulted from their partisan conflicts among themselves. When Augusta was attacked, a body of volunteers from North and South Carolina marched to cooperate with the British in attacking it, four times as large as the whole force that could be raised from the surrounding country to aid General Howe in defending Savannah.

Vigorous efforts were subsequently made by the Americans to recover possession of the state, and although they met with partial successes at certain points in the interior, on the whole their attempts failed, and Georgia remained substantially under British rule until the conclusion of the war.

ATTACK UPON CHARLESTON REPULSED

In the course of the spring of 1780, as soon as the British felt that their possession of Georgia was secure, they sent a strong force along the coast to attack Charleston, as a preliminary step to the subjugation of South Carolina. The enterprise, however, did not succeed. General Lincoln was at this time in command of the American forces at the south, and he was in the interior engaged in gathering and organizing troops, when the British expedition arrived before Charleston. The people of the city, as soon as they heard of the approach of the enemy, engaged vigorously in the work of throwing up fortifications on the land side, and of garrisoning and strengthening the forts that protected the harbor. For a few days after the British troops arrived before the town, and while General Lincoln was making his preparations to come to their aid, they were in imminent danger. But they held their ground with great resolution and spirit, and before the British were prepared for making an assault, General Lincoln arrived with a force much superior to theirs, and they accordingly abandoned the siege and made the best of their way back to Savannah.

A NEW AND GRAND EXPEDITION ORGANIZED

During the summer of 1780 there was no essential change, except that the country appeared to be falling more and more completely under British rule. Great numbers of the people of the interior, especially of the wealthy planters, took the oath of allegiance to the king, and accepted of "protections" from the British generals. Charleston however held out, and General Lincoln still kept the field at the head of a considerable force, which he made every possible effort to increase and strengthen.

At length in the fall of the year, after the sickly season had passed, the British authorities in New York made arrangements for organizing an expedition which they intended should be amply sufficient to secure the accomplishment of the object which they had in view—namely, to capture Charleston and thus complete the subjugation of the whole southern country. Sir Henry Clinton himself took command of the expedition. The fleet, which consisted both of transports for conveying troops and ships of war to cooperate in the attack upon the town, was under the command of Admiral Arbuthnot.

The force which Clinton took with him on this expedition consisted of seven thousand men.

STORMY PASSAGE OF THE FLEET

It was late in the season when the expedition sailed from New York, and the fleet encountered heavy storms, and met with serious disasters on the passage. Some of the vessels were wrecked on the coast. Others that had become separated from the rest were captured by the French or American cruisers that were hovering about in those seas. The fleet was in fact so beaten about and so much damaged that it became necessary to proceed first to Savannah to refit before commencing operations before Charleston.

At length, however, the damages were repaired and the expedition sailed again from Savannah, and arrived off Charleston Harbor in February, 1780. The troops were immediately landed, a camp was formed, and preparations were commenced for advancing upon Charleston.

SLOW ADVANCE OF THE ARMY

The ground being low and level and everywhere intersected by creeks and inlets from the sea, and by swamps and morasses, the operations of the invading army were necessarily much retarded.

Several weeks passed in fact before they actually reached the environs of the city. During all this time the city itself and the whole surrounding country were in a state of great excitement and commotion. Everything possible was done to provide means for defending the place. Slaves were impressed from the surrounding plantations and set at work, under the direction of engineers, to construct fortifications. Old vessels were sunk to obstruct the channels in the rivers at the junction of which Charleston is built, in order to prevent the enemy from taking their ships of war above the

News of peace in camp.

The English, too, were stronger than the French at sea, and the French ships were often exposed to great danger, and sometimes were closely blockaded in an American port, where they even, in certain cases, required an American force to be detained a long time to assist in keeping the British ships out by acting as garrisons to forts and batteries commanding the approaches.

The movements of the French fleets, moreover, on the American coasts, were connected with, and often controlled by, certain operations going on in the West Indies, in which the Americans were not directly interested. From these and various other causes the most that the Americans could do, for one or two years after the conquest of South Carolina and Georgia by the British, even with the help of their powerful allies, was to maintain their ground substantially in the other provinces, without making any decided progress toward expelling the invaders.

LAFAYETTE

Of all the French officers, whether military or naval, who came to America to take part in the contest, the one whose services were most valuable was General Lafayette. He was a young French nobleman possessed of an ample fortune; and not quite nineteen years of age when the news of the declaration of independence by the Americans arrived in Paris, and young as he was, he was at once inspired with a feeling of the warmest and most devoted sympathy for the American cause. At the close of 1776, in what was perhaps the darkest period of our history, he resolved to come to America and personally aid in the contest; and he did so, leaving a young and beautiful wife of high rank and great fortune, to whom he was tenderly attached, and encountering a great deal of difficulty from the opposition made to his plans by the French government and by a wide circle of very influential relatives and friends. He devoted himself fully to the cause during the whole period of the war. An account of his adventures and exploits—the sufferings that he endured and the efforts and sacrifices that he made, would fill volumes, and not even a summary of them can be given here. He will be looked upon by Americans in all coming generations to the end of time, as one of the chief founders of the republic.

ADVANCE OF LORD CORNWALLIS

The reader will recollect that at the close of the last chapter we left Lord Cornwallis in command at the South, with instructions from General Clinton that after having completely re-established the old colonial system in South Georgia and South Carolina, he should march to the northward and reduce North Carolina and Virginia also to subjugation.

In the execution of this plan Cornwallis was engaged quite successfully, on the whole, in 1780 and 1781, in the prosecution of various military operations in North Carolina and Virginia. At length in the summer of 1781, after a series of conflicts and maneuvers in the middle of the State of Virginia, in which he was opposed principally by a force under the command of Lafayette, he gathered his forces together in and around Yorktown—upon a territory which forms a sort of peninsula bounded, as will be seen by the map, by the rivers York and

James, and the waters of Chesapeake Bay—with a view of making that position a base for ulterior and more important operations.

The Position

The position was a very strong one. It was easily accessible from sea by the British ships, being near the entrance of Chesapeake Bay, and thus the most perfect facilities were afforded for receiving reinforcements and supplies. The rivers York and James bordered the territory on the north and south, and formed excellent lines of defense in those directions, while the principal town—Yorktown—which contained all desirable facilities for landing troops, munitions of war and supplies, and also for the storage of goods and for the convenience and comfort of officers and men—was so situated as to be very easily and strongly fortified. Lord Cornwallis considered the position as on the whole combining all the advantages that he could desire, with a view to his future operations.

Washington

While Cornwallis had been forming these plans, and taking possession of his post, Washington had been engaged in preparing for an attack upon New York, in hopes that with the aid of the French, who were now present in America in considerable force, he might recover possession of that city—but on hearing of the position which Cornwallis had taken up in Virginia, he conceived the idea of secretly abandoning his intention of attacking New York, and moving a large part of his force in a stealthy manner to the southward—while the French proceeded thither in the same way by sea—making a show all the time of continuing his preparations to attack New York, so as to keep the English fleets and armies as much as possible in the waters and on the banks of the Hudson. He hoped by this maneuver to be able to surround and capture the whole of Lord Cornwallis's army before the English could send a force to rescue them.

This plan was immediately put into execution, and the stratagem was perfectly successful. So successful, in fact, was Washington in deceiving the English that at one time General Clinton sent orders to Cornwallis to despatch a portion of his troops to New York in order to assist in defending the city from the impending attack of the French and Americans upon it, and the men were actually embarked on board the transports at Yorktown. But on the arrival of a fresh body of Hessians in New York Harbor the order was countermanded.

Difficulties

Although the plan was in the end successful, very great difficulties were to be encountered in carrying it into effect. It required a great deal of nice management and maneuvering to withdraw the troops from the vicinity of New York without exciting the suspicions of the British generals, and many adroit artifices were resorted to for the purpose of deceiving them. The troops too were unwilling to go. Of course their destination and the object which it was intended to accomplish were entirely concealed from them, and when they reached Philadelphia, and learned that they were to go still farther south, they were almost ready to mutiny. Their discontent was greatly increased by their destitute condition and their want of pay. The funds at the disposal of Congress, and the national credit, were both entirely exhausted. The paper money which the government began to issue at the beginning of the war, and which had been their main reliance, had depreciated in value until it became entirely worthless and ceased to be used altogether; and now the only way by which the wants of the soldiers could be so far supplied as to induce them to go on, was by the efforts of private individuals to procure funds in specie. Lafayette himself bought a large quantity of hats, shoes, and other articles of clothing, by means of his own private resources, for the use of his men.

Maneuvering of the Fleets

There were many movements and maneuvers of the French and English squadrons on the coast, the admirals on each side doing all in their power to discover and defeat each other's designs. These movements were connected and complicated with the operations in the West Indies, and with the convoying of fleets of merchantmen. Some collisions and partial conflicts took place, but the French succeeded in August in sending a squadron into the Chesapeake with transports conveying three thousand men. These troops were landed before the British could interfere. They soon formed a junction with the other troops, and all, including those that had been under Lafayette's command before, and those that had been marched from New York by land, amounting to sixteen thousand men, advanced on all the approaches leading to Cornwallis's position, and completely hemmed him in. Cornwallis's force was not more than half as large as that of his besiegers. They were all immediately concentrated in Yorktown and in the immediate environs, and began energetically to prepare for defending themselves there.

The Siege

They succeeded in maintaining their position for several weeks, in hopes that Clinton would send a fleet to rescue them. But the French fleet in the Chesapeake was now so strong that considerable preparation was necessary to fit out an expedition of sufficient magnitude to accomplish the purpose. Clinton urged forward the work as fast as possible, and at length sailed from New York with a formidable fleet, and a force of seven thousand men. But he was too late. When he arrived off the capes of the Chesapeake he learned, to his inexpressible disappointment and chagrin, that Cornwallis had surrendered on the very day that his expedition sailed.

The Surrender

Lord Cornwallis had maintained his position as long as there was any hope, and had tried every possible means of extricating himself from the snare into which he had fallen. But the Americans and French were gaining ground every day. Their incessant cannonading was destroying his ramparts and dismounting his guns, and his own supply of ammunition was nearly exhausted. As a last desperate resort he determined to cross the river, with all his forces, in boats, cut through the American lines, and make his way to New York with the remnant that might escape the slaughter that would inevitably result from such an attempt.

He accordingly provided the boats and made everything ready in the most secret manner, and at ten o'clock one night commenced the passage. The boats went over once, with a portion of the men, but when they were returning a storm of wind and rain arose, so sudden and violent that the boats became entirely unmanageable, and the river, which was here about a mile wide, was turned into a raging sea, rendering all operations upon it with such frail craft utterly impossible.

The consequence was that many of the boats were carried down the river and lost. With the rest it was scarcely possible, after the storm abated a little, to bring back the men who had been taken over. The whole attempt was necessarily abandoned, and it could not be again resumed, since now all was discovered to the Americans, and most effectual measures would of course be taken to prevent any renewal of such an attempt.

No other course was now left to the British commander but to surrender. Articles of capitulation were finally drawn up and signed by both parties, and at an appointed day the whole British army, seven thousand men, marched out, piled their arms and surrendered themselves prisoners of war. Besides these land forces, the British ships that were there, with all the naval stores, and fifteen hundred seamen, were given up to the French admiral.

CONSEQUENCES OF THE SURRENDER OF CORNWALLIS

The surrender of Cornwallis took place on the 17th of October, 1781, and it virtually terminated the war. The treaty of peace, it is true, was not finally concluded until nearly a year after this time, and during the interval the armies on both sides remained in the field, and retained a hostile attitude toward each other; and some minor and comparatively unimportant military movements and operations took place. As soon, however, as the news of the loss of the British army arrived in England, the party there who had been opposed to the war, and had been inclined to take part with the Americans, was rapidly and largely increased, and though the king himself resisted the current as long as he could, there was at length carried in the House of Commons, after an earnest struggle, a vote for an address to his majesty recommending that the war should be stopped. The ministry that had supported the war of course resigned, and the king was compelled to yield.

Peace

The new ministry immediately took measures for negotiating a treaty of peace, and the news was received in the American camps by the war-worn and exhausted soldiers, and among all the towns and villages throughout the country, by the whole population, with unbounded joy.

The people had indeed great occasion to rejoice, for the means and resources of the government for carrying on the war, and even for keeping their armies in the field, were almost entirely gone, and the soldiers in all the camps were reduced nearly to the last stages of destitution and suffering. Still, if the end had not been thus received, the country would have aroused itself to new efforts and continued the struggle.

The position in which the treaty with Great Britain, acknowledging the independence of the United States, placed the country before the world, and the measures which Washington and the other leaders of the revolution adopted to establish and inaugurate a firm and consolidated government for the great people thus, for the first time, taking its place among the nations of the earth, will form the subject of the next and concluding volume of this series.

The End.

Lightning Source UK Ltd.
Milton Keynes UK
UKHW022019030821
388208UK00002B/530